AAE

a
black
GIRLS
guide
to
dating
white
MEN

a
black
GIRLS
guide
to
dating
white
MEN

NIKI MCELROY

Angelic Angels Entertainment, LLC
Publishing division

Angelic Angels Entertainment, LLC
Publishing Dept.
P.O. Box 163226
Sacramento, Ca 90048

Editing by Jake Markel

Book Cover Design by
Richard Rennie

Book cover Photographed by Joel Flora

Male Cover Model
Leonardo Attolini

Library of Congress cataloging -in- Publication Data
McElroy, Niki.
PCN 2011908413

ISBN 9780615490939 (pbk)

Manufactured in the United States of America

www.TheCreamInMyCoffee.com

For my daughters
Cephira Claire
and
Cylia Rose

May you always love with and open heart.

With Special thanks to my Black Girls

Ericka Harden
Nicole Donely
Alyssia Mendez
Tina Divina

Thank you for your inspiration
and support.

CONTENTS

Foreword

By:
Michael Brouillet

*H*aving dated black women and growing up in a 99% white environment, the issues and implications of interracial dating have always been of interest to me. This interest in social phenomena manifested itself into my acquired M.A. from the University of Texas at San Antonio in Sociology with a concentration in power and race. I can't tell you how many of my white friends have confided to me their secret desire to date a black woman. When presented with this information, I usually ask them the same question, "why don't you?" Usually it comes down to either they don't know how to approach black women or they don't know any. Drawing on Niki's background in comedy, "A Black Girls Guide to Dating White Men" is an often humorous and always informative peak into actually bridging the gap between someone being open to interracial dating and actually doing it.

Although the taboo of interracial dating theoretically exists less and less in American society today, the de facto reality is that norms and mores are slow to change. While it is true that interracial black/white marriage has been doubling percentage wise each of the last three decades, it remains the interracial union that has grown the slowest. Black/White marriage is undeniably a very small sliver of the overall marriage composition in the United States. These unions made up a mere .3% of all marriages in 1980 and have only risen to .6% of all marriages by 2000 (Lewis 2010). Total interracial marriages have grown significantly faster, but a large composition of this growth is is made up of hispanic and non-hispanic unions and does not reflect a similar growth trend in black/white unions.

The relative explosion of interracial dating among young people suggests that people are open to dating outside of their race. However, when it comes to marriage, they still marry within. This speaks to the often unspoken reality of racial divide that continues to exist in American society at large.

Niki addresses this divide and has written a witty "how to" book with tips to bridging it. It's one part qualitative sociological analysis, one part racial translation and one part pure humor. Read this book ready to learn, laugh, disagree and discuss.

a
black
GIRLS
guide
to
dating
white
MEN

Let's Get Started...

Chapter One

Introduction:

Why a White Man?

"There aren't enough good Black Men!"
— Every black woman,
at some point in their life.

I AM A BLACK WOMAN
AND I
DATE WHITE MEN

*W*hen my black girlfriends discover the fact that I date white men, they think I'm crazy. They don't understand what a white man has to offer a black woman and why I would continuously choose to date melanin deficient males. Their main concerns were what money, sex and power play in interracial dating and if it's worth giving it a try. So I was inspired to write this book.

Among these pages I will give you the answers to those taboo questions that I know you've been dying to ask, gleaned from my years of field work. Whether you laugh in glee, groan in despair or take offense, at the end of the day this is my story. So sit back, relax and learn from my mistakes, triumphs and revelations. And hell, now I can say I'm a published author an that's a resume builder to get me more quality white dates. Hope you're taking notes!

The first time I heard my mother tell a friend, "There aren't enough good black men" I wondered why she was looking for a "black man" as opposed to a "man". As I grew in age and yes, experience, I went through MANY MANY MANY dating experiences (did I mention MANY?). Realizing I was becoming somewhat of a specialist in this field, I began to notice a trend. Each culture offers it's own unique stereotypical traits. And, dear reader, I don't "generalize". I prefer to say that I "stereotype", only because it makes the dating game easier.

MANY TYPES OF LOVERS

First, I went through a Latin stage when the faces of Antonio Banderas, Enrique Iglesias and Ricky Martin began to grace my screen. I wanted, even needed, a Latin Lover. They were sensual, giving, compassionate and nothing was better than hearing them say, just about anything, with that sexy, tongue rolling accent. My Latin Lover could bark, "Woman, make me a sandwich" and in a puppy like trance I'd prance happily into the kitchen (cue eye-roll).

However, there comes a day in any relationship, when a couples "sweetheart phase" fades and you have your first disagreement. This is where you find out the ugly side of your partner. Let me tell you, it can't get any uglier than being in the line of fire between a Latin man and Black woman. It's quite the scene. The Fiery Latin and the "What did you say to me? Who do you think you are mutha fucka?" Black woman, battling over the land of Control. Neither one will back down, and the great sex after every fight will keep a black woman there longer than planned. Inevitably the roller coaster will come to a jolting stop.

I have also found that this type of battle occurs often with other cultures that are typically known to have dominant men. I've tried my hand with Persians, Pakistanians, Spaniards and quite a few in between. Black women and these men share a lot of common ground when it comes to goals and family expectations, but we just can't seem to agree on who will be the head of the household.

EASTERN HEMISPHERE

I even gave had a gander Eastern hemisphere. These are all Asian countries, including India. This contraction of yellow fever led me to intelligent on the whole, and one could learn a lot from them. With the asian men that I have dated, cultural tradition has been very important, and something about that quality has always attracted me, maybe because we lack that here in America. Somehow, the Asian culture has been able to keep these priceless qualities instilled in their families, generation after generation. And remain particularly intrigued by Japanese men as my quest for the right match continues.

There was a time in my life when all I wanted was an Indian wedding and a part of me still does. If you haven't seen one, rent the movie *Monsoon Wedding*, a beautiful film that depicts the traditional Indian wedding. They are beautiful: the henna, the marigold flowers, the dancing, the jewels. Everything would look to be perfect. The men are great and love their wives and families completely, but one, small factor would ruin it all. The sex is bad. Or atleast in my humble (connisseur's) experience. It's not that I've been with a slew of Indian men, but if 5 out of 5 had the same "tired" moves, I will not give mister 6 a chance. If I went to Bebe and bought 5 pairs of jeans and they all ripped the second day of wearing them, I would be an idiot to buy another. It would be a waste of time and effort.

And there is also the issue of arranged marriages. That certainly strikes me as a risky deal. Thats like the Americans that wait for marriage to move in together. I personally need a test run. No california "Lemon Law" can protect you from that type of travesty.

We know the best way to tell someones ability in bed is by the way they move on the dance floor. So, here's the problem; they can't dance. Sure, their form of dance is a bit different than ours. It's typically a jump and a hop sort of thing. I have a great time doing it when heavily intoxicated but rhythm comes naturally to black women. You can see it in the way we walk down the street as if we hear the drums of our ancestors banging away as we hit each step right on beat with our hips swaying from side to side. In life, just as on the dance floor, we need someone who can handle us at the right times, and who lets us take the lead when we feel it's our turn. We need someone who understands our emotions and lets us vent when we need to blow our top; someone who can literally hold our asses down in bed. We want someone strong enough to break down our emotional walls even if our wall tells us we don't. Who would be best to understand us and our struggles?

THE BLACK MAN

This leads me to the question of whether black men can live up to this ideal. I do love my Chocolaty Lovers so this book is not meant to degrade them and their capacities in any way. They just don't do "IT" for me. I feel something is, was, or always has been lost; maybe from the great lack of father figures in American black culture. These are the men that we are stuck with.

I've dated all types of black men, from professional athletes, rappers, singers, doctors, lawyers, architects and every other field imaginable. There were some awesome men in each group, however, when it came to love, dates and courtship, they showed zero effort. In my experience, when dealing with the average black man, this attitude has been a common issue that many black women have had to deal with. White women on the other hand? A whole other story and a whole other book.

I have many black male friends who have great women chasing them and I don't see why they can't try harder to show these women the appreciation they deserve and make an effort to treat them as the queens that they are. Going back to my mothers line, "There aren't enough good black men" and unfortunately, black men know it! Well, if they're going to take unfair advantage of this situation, why not open our doors to other "styles" of good men?

My friends have asked me many questions over the years, so I decided to compile the answers into a book in order to help other black women who are considering crossing over to the "white side".

If a white man can meet your ultimate goals in the long run, is it really that bad? If I can answer the questions you have and show you the possible benefits, would you be willing to give it a try?

This book is an easy, user friendly guide to dating white men. Once again, this book is based on my own personal experiences and research. I'm not saying that there aren't any exceptions to the opinions I'll outline here. However, I have picked up on the most common patterns to dating white men and now I will share them with you. Behold, *A Black Girls Guide to Dating White Men*.

Chapter Two

Where to Find a White Man

"There are much easier things in life
than finding a good man...
Nailing Jell-O to a tree, for instance."
—Author Unknown

WHAT TYPE OF MAN
FLOATS YOUR BOAT
AND
WHAT OCEAN IS HE IN?

*F*inding a good man is difficult, but now that you're considering opening your doors to a new race, your opportunities have increased tremendously. There are many good white men out there for you to sink your claws into.

When changing your dating style, in any way, be it class or career, you have to change your outlook and your behaviors. You can catch a bee with honey, a dog with a bone and a fly with shit. You mix those around and you'll catch nothing.

The same theory can also be applied to men. You've got to decide what type of white man you want. Do you want an attorney? Do you want the athletic man that you can catch on the basketball court with friends, every Saturday morning? Or are you looking for the guy that you can be artistic with? By starting with that decision, it will make your search a bit easier and you can make your fine tuning adjustments from there. Be aware, it's a tough decision to make because each has their own unique qualities. But if you know who you are and have an understanding of what you want for yourself, you'll figure out which will be the best fit for you.

If you are not sure what type of white guy you're looking for, or where to find him:

* this is the chapter for you! Move to the next page

If you already have your eyes on that certain someone:

* skip to chapter 3 where we get down to business.

THE BUSINESS MAN

Sean McCracken

The business man is the fast talking, money throwing, elbow rubbing, luxury car driving class act. He enjoys great meals and likes his women like his credit card, black and easily accessible. Okay, the last part I just wrote to sound good but a wealthy business man really wants to have an attractive and classy woman on his arm. If you are sexy and you get a lot of stares, he wants you with him.

"Mr. GQ" doesn't have a lot of spare time on his hands so he likes a woman that isn't too busy. He works long hours and when he has a little time off, he wants to spend that time having a great time with you. If you are in school or working long hours then the time you can spend together will be limited and he'll find someone else to occupy his time, whether he is still with you or not. If you have kids, you must have good childcare available 24/7 and they must allow last minute drop off's.

When I complained to an attorney friend of mine that he was working too much, his response was, "I need to make money so I can afford to take you out." He then proceeded to tell me this joke; "A boy had a date planned so he went to the gym and asked his trainer what machine he should use to impress the girl. The trainer told him to use the ATM machine outside of the gym."

Businessmen are aware that they can get a better quality of woman with the money that they make, hence their obsession with making money.

If you're independent and can deal with his slight cockiness, the business man is a great catch for a woman who loves excitement and the finer things in life. He just may not be there all the time to enjoy it with you.

THE JOCK

Tyler Haines

The jock is the fun good old boy that you can hang out and relax with. He is the man that most of us are used to. He probably was a high school quarter back, finished a few years of college and quit because of better work opportunities. He is typically the blue collar hard worker, stays in shape and loves Monday night football with the boys.

The jock is good with his hands so he is helpful around the house and knows how to fix things. You can expect him to be home at a decent hour and handle husband/fatherly duties. With this kind of man, unless he is part businessman, you can expect an American middle class to upper middle class life; 2.5 kids and a dog.

This white man is adventurous and you can find them surfing, sky diving and playing in all other x-game styled sports. You may even catch him at the local park jumping into a pick up game of basketball. Just as they are with sports, they are in the bed, you will have a wild and crazy time with them.

Your jock may need help dressing to your standards, but that's a task that most of us women enjoy and when you're done, he will look sexy and presentable.

If you are a laid back, easy going girl who likes to dress down and play sports on occasion, the jock is the boy for you. He offers stability and reliability.

THE EDGY DUDE

Chris Aquila

You may have seen the edgy dude hanging out at the tattoo shops or maybe you have walked by them on the street. These guys are typically covered in tats, piercings and have a clothing style like no other.

Society has had names for these guys in the past decades. They have been called punks or bad boys and they'd be the boys that your parents would dread for you to bring home. These days, their style is seen as hot and sexy. Women love these laid back, artsy kinds of guys because their edginess makes you feel like you are living on the wild side.

The truth behind this hard exterior is that the edgy boys are the most artistic which is displayed through paintings, music or writing. They spend many hours creating, envisioning and applying their masterpieces.

Most of their careers deal with public service. Be it a barber, a bartender, musician or any other job that allows them to meet new creative people and keep them in the public eye. These boys take pride in how their style projects them, right down to the accessories and shoes.

Your edgy dude, is extremely loving and thoughtful. Just as hard as their exterior is, is how soft they are inside, for their friends, family and ladies that they they care about.

If you like to party like a rockstar and love a downtown styled man with a heart of gold, the edgy dude is the white boy for you!

GO WHERE YOUR TYPE OF WHITE GUY IS.

Now that you have chosen your dream guy, you may ask, "Well, where do I find them?" If you're looking for a white man, hanging out at a NAACP cocktail dinner won't maximize your options. You'll get a few, but chances are, you're not the only black woman with eyes on him. You want to put yourself in situations where the ratios are in your favor.

You must leave your comfort zone, and try something new. If that means attending a play or an event that you may have never thought of attending before, do so. If you are not comfortable around too many white people, take a caucasian girlfriend with you, to make you feel more at ease. As a black woman, you'll look more approachable if you are sitting alone because white men will feel more inclined to start a conversation if you're not already in a deep conversation with a friend. He may feel that he is intruding. So, if you do decide to bring a friend, make sure you bring an outgoing, socially conscious one, to help you break the ice.

There are many different locations white men frequent. I find that they are a creature of habit, so if there is a place that they enjoy, you can catch them there over and over again. If neither of you had the courage to speak to each other the first time, go again, and get him the next time!

Here is a list of locations that I find worthy of frequenting which can provide many new date potentials.

UPSCALE RESTAURANTS AND BARS

An upscale restaurant or a bar located inside or near a 4-5 star hotel is where you can find the business man and a sprinkle of jocks. It's full of upper middle class to wealthy singles eating dinner alone. They probably dine there often and know the wait staff by name.

The men that frequent these places are typically business men who love to travel, experience great things, eat fabulous food and generally, have an appreciation for the finer things in life. Some may be there on a business trip and looking for someone to spend time with while they're in town.

I tend to like the travelers, because I feel that this gives me the opportunity to meet more men than just the ones that live in my city. This is a perfect opportunity for you ladies that live in small towns. Whoever said long distance relationships don't last, obviously didn't know about frequent flyer miles! If this is the type of man that you are looking for, you have chosen the perfect location.

White men don't typically cook for themselves and would rather go out while still enjoying a lovely dinner with a desirable ambiance. That isn't to say that they do know how to cook. They just feel its a waste of time and effort to cook for one. They'd much rather head out into a social environment where they will have the opportunity to make the acquaintance of someone like you. So when you meet them there, here are a few tips to heighten your chances of making a love connection in an upscale establishment.

TIP #1
DRESS APPROPRIATELY
FOR THE
ESTABLISHMENT.

Sometimes you may not be too sure about what to wear to that certain establishment that you heard the CEO's talking about in the office. All it takes is one phone call to the hostess of the restaurant and they can tell you the dress code. With the advanced technology we have now, you can even go online and see photos of people dining in that particular location.

Be sure to look professional and yet, sexy, at the same time. Even if your career doesn't necessarily call for a professional look, throw it on before you head out. Remember, this is where your businessmen will be hanging out and you want to entice them to approach you instead of the girl sitting next to you.

Throw a sexy, low cut, top underneath a blazer and pump up your makeup to a "night" look by adding a brighter lipstick or adding a little darker eyeshadow to your lids. This will be the accentuation needed to bring your white man over with a drink. Keep in mind, one

If I didn't do my research on the attire for the
Del Mar Horse Races, I could have looked like a
disaster.

thing we don't want to do is feed into the stereotype that some may have seen grace their television screens. The hootchie mama short skirts with shoes that strap all the way to the thigh. Yes, there are the white men that are attracted to that look, but the ones in this particular type of establishment generally are looking for a more professional type, at least while out in public. They are looking for the type of woman that they are comfortable bringing to a dinner meeting for work.

TIP #2
BE WILLING
TO
DRIVE ACROSS TOWN.

Depending on your location, you may have to drive away from your neighborhood to find the perfect establishment full of successful, single white men who are looking for love. Although you may be nervous, you will have to move out of our comfort zone if you want to succeed. You can't expect to get different results while repeating the same old actions. I suggest visiting the wealthiest area in your town. If you live in Los Angeles, go straight to Beverly Hills! Don't waste your time in Hollywood, where it's hit or miss. Finer restaurants = Finer men. By "Fine" I don't necessarily mean the looks. I mean the education level, the career level and of course, the money level. If your looking for a business man, it's where you'll need to be.

When dating, you should want to find the best of the best, and when it comes to dating white men, you should keep to those same standards, if not higher. By choosing a classier restaurant with food made freshly in the back and not just defrosted, you are now setting the standard that you will not accept anything less, that is, at least during the courting process. We all love a little Red Lobster or Sizzlers every now and again, but not on a first date!

TIP #3
IF YOU DON'T HAVE MONEY, ORDER WATER WITH LIME. (IT WILL LOOK JUST LIKE A VODKA SODA!)

Remember, the more you get out, the better your chances at finding a white guy that you click with, so don't let the mere fact of being broke deter you. Walk in to the bar with confidence. If it makes you feel better, have a "story" in your head, that maybe you aren't drinking tonight and are just waiting for your friend who, of course, conveniently cancels on you. Maybe you are waiting for traffic to die down before heading home, or possibly killing time before your movie begins. Please, make sure you actually have a film and time available, just in case the man you end up talking to buys you a couple drinks and then wants to join you at the theater.

If you do want to fork out $12 a drink, remember to drink responsibly. Nothing is worse than getting drunk when first meeting someone and not actually remembering the conversations or ever even meeting them in the first place. These words are spoken from experience.

There are men that I have found in my phone that I don't actually remember ever getting their number. But when I've Googled their names, they have been gorgeous white guys! Yes, I have called them up to a year later and YES they've remembered me. It's not often men of this caliber have the chance to talk to black women and it's never too late to follow up on a missed opportunity.

TIP #4
STAY OFF OF YOUR PHONE

A habit that many people fall victim to, including myself, is having your phone as a companion. Just be aware that by keeping your head buried into your phone while out eating alone, you are slimming your chances for making that "love connection" through eye contact.

Sometimes, we feel a bit vulnerable sitting alone, so we will play on Facebook, text, and do everything we can to look busy. We may even start Mapquesting locations we aren't even planning on visiting, just to appear that we have something important going on. We need to learn to live in the moment and pick up on the energy that is around us.

This rule applies to everyone. Whether you are looking for the businessman, the jock or the edgy dude. If you think of how many missed connections that you may have had due to being absorbed in technology, you'd want to toss all your "i's", like your ipod, ipad and iphone. Put that energy back into your real eyes, look up and notice your opportunities.

ATHLETIC AND COUNTRY CLUBS

Another place to find single white men of all types is at the gym. They love to work out. At least, the ones that look good and care about their health do and those are the ones you should want.

As black women, we tend shy away from the gym, due to our hair. It's not that we don't want to work out, we just don't want to deal with the process afterwards. One solution is to just put on your cutest workout clothes and sit at the protein shake bar, no one said that you actually had to go there and sweat.

If the idea of hanging around moist and stinky men makes you cringe go to your local country club instead. Many business men go to country clubs for their unofficial business meetings on the golf course. You can find them at the country club bar after their round. Here are tips to help you find and attract men at frequent the athletic/country clubs.

TIP #1
TRY SOMETHING NEW

Actor, Travis Aaron Wade, and I met at a celebrity golf tournament and remain close friends.

If you are athletic, and even if you're not, try to play golf! It is fun, relaxing and actually makes a great date. It's something that a lot of black women don't do, and because many of us are naturally athletic, I think it's something that we would be as good at, if not better, than the women currently dominating the WPGA.

You're going to want to find a way into a "Private" golf course, if you're looking for a more "exclusive" type of business man. The way into this type of facility is by either getting a membership or by being invited by a member. There is a strict dress code and you may need to go shopping before you head out there. You can also find out what the clubs dress code by checking online or by calling.

If you have older white men around you, be it a regular customer, a co-worker or an employer, let them know that you are interested in going to the club and more often than not, they will extend an invite. Most will assume that you are not interested so it's up to you to let them know that you are. Even many black men have memberships because they realize that it is a great way to build rapport with other business men, so try asking your uncle or your friends aunt's boyfriend's sister's cousin. He just may have a hookup.

TIP #2
VISIT DIFFERENT GYMS

Visit different athletic clubs and parks to see which place has more men that pique your interest. Different clubs offer different types of men to choose from. Some cater more to the business men, some have more of the basketball playing/athletic white men and some just have the aerobic jazzersizers.

You can go to each for free by asking for a one or two week pass. Most clubs are willing to offer the pass to you, for a potential membership. So use this opportunity to check out the gyms and clubs in your neighborhood as well as neighborhoods outside of your area. Remember, we are still working to get outside of our comfort zones and into new areas.

TIP #3
GO TO THE GYM
DIFFERENT
TIMES OF THE DAY.

People pick their gym time based on their daily schedules and routines. That said, if you are looking to date a business professional try to go to the gym before 8am and after 5pm. On the other hand, if you are looking for a man with a more flexible schedule and/or career, like the edgy dude, go in the mid morning–early afternoon.

Going at different times will give you many options in men. You'll typically see the same men there at the same times every day.

NIGHTCLUBS AND HOLE IN THE WALLS

What better way to meet your white man than with him dosed up on plenty of "liquid courage". Yes, you're probably going to hate the house / rock / techno country music in the establishment, but just remember, you can always reprogram the radio in their cars later. Or teach yourself to enjoy a little Coldplay, John Mayer or James Blunt. It's actually pretty good music and you

Ericka Harden and Leonardo Attolini

may find yourself liking it better than this new wave of 21st century Hip Hop. I know I do.

I personally prefer to meet my men in what is called a "hole in the wall" bar. They are small, more intimate and tend to have a lot of the same patrons who attend regularly. Here, you will find mostly jocks and edgy dudes, with a sprinkle of down to earth business men.

For myself, if I get too wild in a "hole in the wall", I'm not going to be as embarrassed the next day. An added bonus to the Hole in The Wall is that everyone there will know your name and will know that you are interested in white guys. Once that is known, it makes it easier for them to ask you out, without their fear of racial rejection.

In the Hole in The Wall, you can get a game of pool, darts, or foosball going, or you can have a quiet chat in the corner. The drinks are cheaper and the crowd is relaxed. Which leads me to nightclubs.

Nightclubs are a different scene all together. You can find white men in these places, but unless they're there for a special event, you may not want to waste your time. It takes a lot of effort from all women in this scene, let alone the black chick looking for a white guy.

Once again, you want the men/women ratios to be in your favor. Even more so, you want the white men/women ratios to be in your favor.

FRIENDS OF FRIENDS

Make sure you let everyone know that you are interested in dating outside of your race. Friends at work and/or school will probably step in with a list full of candidates. Everyone loves to play matchmaker in these situations.

Be sure to let your friends and family know that you aren't looking for just any white guy. Black people sometimes assume that there is no difference and if you'll date one white guy, you'll date them all.

Tanisha:
Hey, there's this white boy at my job I want to hook you up with. He's cute!

Niki:
The one that just got out of prison?

Remember, black or white, you still have standards!

ONLINE

Many black women and white men have found love online, successfully. This is the new wave of being social, which in my personal opinion, is just the opposite of being social. so I need more research in this department. Many matches are made from online services.

I prefer to meet my men in person because I find that they always look different than their photos and there is nothing like real eye contact to develop a connection. Although, if I met them while I am drunk they always look different than they do without my beer goggles. So you can win either way.

If you do decide to start online dating, there are many sites dedicated solely to interracial relationships and they can be found with a simple search. Many are paid sites, but internet dating can be an easy way to reach outside of your area without any real effort.

Just remember, whether online or with beer goggles, be safe.

Chapter Three

There's More than just our Looks

"God gave us all a penis and a brain,
but only enough blood to run one at a time."
—Robin Williams

UPDATE YOUR LOOKS LIKE YOU UPDATE YOUR FACEBOOK STATUS ... STAY CURRENT

*T*here have been studies done that prove many white men ultimately choose a mate by beauty and not by race. I have met many that find black women beautiful and sexy. And for the record, the #1 buyer of black porn are white men!

But ladies, sometimes I'm left to wonder who the hell dressed you or what clown school did your makeup. Dressing up does not always mean matching eyeshadow to your dress. As a matter of fact, it NEVER does! I am a MAC Cosmetics fan, it's where I worked for 5 years, but sometimes the workers there give everyday people a little too much artistic flare.

It seems as though many black women get their sense of beauty from fashion couture models and bootilicious video vixens. FYI, not even the video vixens wear their makeup that heavy and bold when they're off camera.

C'mon ladies, make it look natural! When meeting your man, you want to look like you are wearing no makeup at all. Be a Covergirl or Revlon natural beauty.

We want the white men to understand that we are naturally beautiful and don't need to cover it with mounds of illusions. What we WILL do is accentuate what we have to its classiest form.

FACE TIME

The first thing a man will notice when you walk into a room is your body, next stop and most important, is your face. There are many things that women can do to make herself look aesthetically appealing, no matter what flaws or blemishes you may have.

TIP #1
FOUNDATION

First we will begin with the skin. You want to make sure that you start with a moisturized surface to allow for a smooth application of foundation, preferably with a brush. Adding a light foundation to even out your skin tone will give you the illusion of "flawless" skin. I know a lot of my ladies in the South tend to shy away from foundations, but like to use every other product. That's like painting without a canvas, there's nothing to hold the picture together.

For those scared of a little foundation, there is a product called a Tinted Moisturizer. This type of moisturizer is a light facial moisturizer, usually with sun protection, that comes in different shades. This will give the illusion of having "flawless" skin to the ladies that don't normally wear foundation. You can find tinted moisturizers at your local makeup counter and is your drug store's beauty department.

Matching foundation can be a pretty difficult process with brown skin. Sometimes they are too red, too yellow, too light or too dark. It will take time and patience for you to find the perfect color and product match for you and your skin, but once you find it, write down the number and never lose it. A great color match should blend perfectly and will not leave a line of demarcation around your jaw line and forehead.

In the summer time my forehead gets darker than the rest of my face. This creates the need for me to purchase a darker color foundation in addition to the lighter foundation that I already use. I use the two colors, dark and light, until the rest of my face catches up in color, after which I then switch to just the darker color.

A "winter" shade and a "summer" shade of foundation is a MUST! We all change colors, no matter how much we dodge the sun.

A great product should not dry, burn or breakout the skin. Most counters are great at making samples that you can use for a week to see how your skin will react to that particular product. So grab a few and have fun.

TIP #2
EYES

When dealing with the eyes, if not professionally trained, stay basic. It's too easy to go wrong. There are many places that can teach you a natural look, but if you're heading out before you have the opportunity to make an appointment, GO BRONZE on the lids!! For the lighter skin, do lighter bronzed and the darker skin, go darker. Try to stay in your skin tone to allow the bronzer to look like a healthy glow.

Next grab a chocolate color, a little darker than your skin to add to the crease of your eyelid. Blend blend blend. There is nothing worst than seeing a dark line across a woman's lid. When you blend your colors at all edges, it makes a softer transition into the next color (meaning your skin color).

TIP #3
THE SMOKEY EYE

Another option is the smokey eye, which will take training and practice before I suggest going out in public. This look is a great one for nightclubs or anytime that you are looking for a glamour styled look.

After starting with your basic eye, you have two options, depending on the shape of your lid. You can choose to add your dark color, dark grey or black, depending on your skin tone, to your eye lid, or the crease of your eye lid.

If you don't have a lot of lid, you can opt to add the dark to your crease, and place a lighter color on your lid. I have seen this done beautifully by other artists and models. But this look, to me, must have false lashes added, unless your lashes are naturally long, thick and fabulous.

I like to add my dark color right on the lid, add a lighter color to the crease (more flesh toned) and blend outward until you can't see the colorline fade. This gives a softer prettier smokey eye.

TIP #4
WORKING WITH COLOR

So you say you like color? I'm not against color, just as long as its done right. When working with colors, remember, just a hint is all that you need. There is no need to cover the entire lid. Using too much will take focus away from your natural beauty. When someone looks at your beautifully shaped eyes, they shouldn't think BLUE!

I suggest adding a hint of blue around the eye line in conjunction with your dark brown or black and bringing it all the way in and around the tear duct area. Opt to not lather on your full lid but, if you do, please blend it outwards. There's nothing worse than seeing a woman with blue caked on her lid and nothing else. If you're going to do it, do it right.

I understand that some woman have a tendency to see a color that they like and want to just go ahead and wear it. Honey, just because you like it, doesn't mean the color is right for you. When in doubt, please seek professional assistance.

Once you've finished your eyeshadow application, don't forget to add your black liner and mascara. If you wear them, fake lashes, can be a great addition to the natural look. Like everything else though, keep things simple.

TIP #5
LIPS

The lips are one of the features that most attracts white men to black women. Our soft pillows need to be cared for with Chapstick or Vaseline daily, to help with peeling issues that may occur while wearing your favorite lip color.

As black women, we can get away with almost any color, except stay away from pale or pasty colors and frosts. Those are the colors that make your lips look ashy and the "I just ate a powdered doughnut" look just isn't sexy.

If you are going with a colorful or smokey look on your eye then it's better to stay away from a bright color lip. If you are doing a smokey eye, stay with light, more natural colors, as you see in the photos with blue eyeshadow. The goal is to accentuate one feature at a time so as not give your white guy sensory overload.

WARDROBE READY

The thought of changing your style to get a man will probably make some of you just give up on the idea of dating a white man. Before you give up, remember that you don't necessarily need to be someone that you're not, but some of you do have to be willing to make some adjustments. Don't forget, he will be making adjustments in order to be with you, too.

Men, in general, are highly attracted to effeminate creatures. They want a "trophy" wife. That woman that makes their friends jealous. Ken wants his Barbie. Well, in our case Ken wants Barbie's black friend, Christie. So, you'll need to dress classy if you expect to have a distinguished white man approach you for relationship purposes. Always wear a dress or skirt to get their attention, but keep an eye on the length. The extra cushion some of us tote around can sometimes make the back of the skirt a little shorter than the front.

When I was in Catholic school, our skirts had to be below our fingertips when our arms were straight down at our sides. Yes, we shrugged our shoulders up a bit, but it still left our assets covered. I always use this as my "rule of thumb" or as I like to call it, my "rule of fingertips".

When getting dressed or shopping for a new wardrobe, lean towards upscale looking items. The key word there is upscale "looking". Just because it looks like you've spent a million bucks, doesn't mean that you did. Living in a larger city, like LA, I'm able to find great trendy items, always on sale. You can catch me

bargaining on Melrose, hitting the fashion district on a Saturday morning or checking the red tags at the Beverly Center boutique shops. But when I lived in Sacramento, a smaller city located in Northern California known as a "cow town", it wasn't quite as easy.

The first place I'd look was the Nordstrom sale rack. Their items offer quality and longevity. Certain times of the year they have amazing discounts and if you buy smart, many items can be worn year round.

The next stop I'd make would be either Nordstrom Rack, the Macy's sale racks, Ross or Marshalls. Once again, if you do your research on the items that you're looking for, most likely you'll find it in one of these shops.

The must have items that should be in your closet are:

* Sexy black skirt and blazer set
* Hot sexy shoes
* A plethora of jewelry options
* Cute, fitted for your body type, jean
* A few sexy low cut blouses
* Black cocktail dress

Now, these are just the basics for grabbing your business man or jock. As you're able to add to your closet you can buy more sexy cocktail dresses and start playing with seasonal colors or different cuts.

I know many women lose and gain weight over the course of a lifetime but, whatever the case, make sure you update these key items so that they are always available to fit you as you are today.

If you have gained weight and are uncomfortable with your size, lose weight! If you are a newly voluptuous woman and you like it, learn what style of the basic items fit your new body type and strut your stuff.

My girlfriend is a size 14/16 and just like Marilyn Monroe, you would never know because of the way that she dresses her curves to accentuate the appropriate areas.

A white man, like any man, loves a woman with confidence, whether she's a size 4 or 14. If you don't love how you look and feel good about yourself, nobody else will or, maybe they do, but you'll never believe them.

A WARDROBE FOR FUN

If you're just looking for a good time with your edgy dude, or a quick romp in the sheets with a business man, the shorter your skirt, the better. When considering a top, the deeper the plunge the more the fun! There really are no rules when playing the "fun" game. Your edgy dudes love this look and it makes them come running.

Whether you decide to dress up or you opt for the fun look is fine, as long as it's feminine.

I have experimented with both. The key is to know what you're looking for whether that's a long term relationship with an edgy dude or just a fun night with a business guy or jock. Get dressed for it, know that that's the decision you are making and go for it. It doesn't necessarily mean it'll end in a quick sexual relationship, but don't go into it thinking that it will be anything more. If it does... bonus!

THE
"PLEASE DONT'S"

When making your clothing choices there are universal NO-NO's that you you must not make. These little things can ruin even the most perfect outfit.

The first are PANTY LINES. This is when you can see the outline of your panties through your skirt, dress or pants. It is NEVER okay for these to be visible. If you are opposed to thongs or get infections easily, opt for a full brief. Make sure that they not too small, as they will cut into your skin, causing a visible line. Another option is a body shaper like Spanx.

Next on the list are the LOVE HANDLES. If you have a few extra pounds, or even if you don't but wear hip huggers that are too tight, you are bound to have a muffin top from your love handles. These are the fat pockets around your waist that love to hang over your clothing.

If you are prone to showing love handles, consider wearing less fitted clothing and higher waisted bottoms.

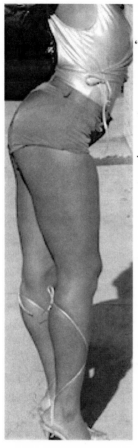

Low hip huggers are not for everyone, no matter how "trendy" you want to be.

Another don't is the hootchie mama booty short that slides in your butt, leaving your vagina looking like it resembles a camal's toe. Business men, jocks and edgy dudes may love this at home, but don't try to wear it to the company picnic or family pool party. If you have an amazing shape, it may look decent, but will never be considered classy.

Strap up shoes are made for the strip club. If you work at one, and you wear strap up shoes, make sure that they do not cut into your legs and look like a pot roast in it's wrapping. If you have a pair of lace up shoes, cut the laces and don't allow them to go higher than the calf. Try to keep the tie focused around the ankle.

GROOMING

I can't move on to the next chapter without talking grooming, and the lack there of, in our community. Some of us know how important this is and this chapter is not for you. Feel free to move on forward. As for the rest of you ladies, you are gorgeous and beautiful just the way you are, but the hair on your body isn't.

I understand that, as women, we go through hormone changes throughout life that can lead to higher levels of testosterone. This may cause hair to grow in unwanted places. Just because you didn't go get hormone replacements doesn't mean that it is acceptable to walk around with hair growing out of your upper lip and chin. PLUCK-WAX, PLUCK-WAX, PLUCK-WAX!! If you can afford it, get laser treatments! Pain is beauty because of just that; IT'S BEAUTIFUL! I've seen amazingly beautiful black women and I get up close, only to see strands of curly facial hair under their chin. It ruins the whole package. Just the thought of it makes me vomit in my mouth.

This leads me to my next point. I speak directly to the ladies who think we're still in the old days of feminism when I say this. Hairy legs are OUT! If you decide to leave them unshaven, please wear nylons in public and leave them on while in bed with your new white man. You can just cut a hole in the crotch, so your hairy, bushy, sweaty, bacteria filled vagina can be accessible. If he enjoys getting scrubbed by a Brillo pad, he may still hit it! Don't even consider putting on a swimsuit. The hairs escaping out of the sides of your suit are not a pleasant sight. A trim is needed for the sake of others sanity.

While working at the Playboy mansion during a casting we found that, out of over 300 contestants, less than ten of them had any hair on their lady parts at all. Most women are going bald down there. Of course, even the ones that had hair kept it groomed properly.

In no way am I suggesting that you have to look like a twelve year old pre-pubestic girl to get a man, I just want to open your eyes to the new trends.

For those of you looking for options for hair removal, whether for your face or body, there are many ways that you can do it. Here is what I have found that has worked for myself or close friends of mine.

SHAVING

* An easy and effective way to remove hair.
* Buy new blades often.
* Make sure the blade is not dull, in order to reduce the chances for razor bumps.
* May cause a darker shadow in the area, due to the hair left in the follicle.
* Hair tends to grow back in 1-2 days.

PLUCKING

* A bit more painful than shaving, but it pulls the hair from the cuticle, eliminating the razor bump and the darker surface area.

* After plucking a few times, you will get used to he pain and it will no longer hurt.
* To help diminish the pain try taking a hot shower first, and moisturize. It'll open the pores to allow for easier extraction.
* Hair tends to grow back in 3-4 weeks.

WAX

* You can buy over the counter wax or go have it done in the shop by a licensed esthetician.
* It can be painful, but it is quick.
* It get less painful with each visit.
* Hair tends to grow back in 3-4 weeks.

THREADING

Our friends from India have brought us this great way of removing hair with thread and the swift hands of your beautician.

* Makes clean brows with defined lines.
* Pain level is a bit intense but, like the others, you will get used to it.

LASER TREATMENTS

* The treatments aren't too painful and the effects are permanent.
* You will no longer have to worry about hair growing in the treated areas.

* You will have to go to a few appointments for
    full hair removal and the price tag is steep. (The
    cost of razors over the course of your life can be
    steep too.)
* I also noticed a friend's armpits that used to have a
    darker pigment where she shaved, got an even tone
    after laser treatments.

Whichever method you decide to follow, do it
regularly and consistently. Whether you're shaving or
making your laser appointments, it will give you smooth
chocolatey skin that looks touchable and inviting. Don't
be a porcupine.

Chapter Four

The Approach

"The tragedy of machismo is that a man
is never quite man enough."
—Germaine Greer

I LOOK GOOD...
NOW WHAT?

So you've located the white men, you've put on the correct attire. Now you may be wondering why you have not been approached by one. Or why the "right" one has not come and swept you off of your feet. It's not that they are not interested, it actually may be quite the opposite.

Mathew, Caucasian, from Texas, who dates black women regularly and holds a Masters degree in Sociology, told me a story about when his best friend got married. While at the Bachelor party, he asked him, "Do you have any regrets?" The friend's response threw Mathew for a spin when he replied, "My only regret is that I never dated a black girl." Mathew was in shock, because in all of the years that he knew this friend, he had never heard him mention being attracted to or wanting to date a black woman. "He never showed any interest in black women," Mathew said.

If this is the story of a "red neck" in Texas, this leads me to believe its the story of many other white men as well. Many of them aren't given too many opportunities to fraternize with black women and, when they do , they lack the confidence to go in for the kill. They fear that they may be rejected in a loud and embarrassing way because we may not like a little creme in our coffee. He may also feel this attraction is crossing a racial barrier and he's sure about how you will react to his pursuit.

THE ANGRY BLACK WOMAN

As Black women, we are known to be strong, confident and opinionated creatures. I won't forget to mention, loud. Mostly inherited from our mothers and grandmothers, these personality traits have been passed down for generations. However, there are also many other rumors about our personalities that put fear in the eyes of a white man.

I've personally met some black women, possessors of those "crazy" attributes. We call them the "Angry Black Women". They do exist and hopefully you are not one of them. The only people who enjoy being around an "Angry Black Woman" are other "Angry Black Women". Misery loves company.

If that is you and you find yourself complaining about things more often than not, arguing for the sake of arguing and looking for things to be wrong in ANY situation, the first step to fixing your problem is acknowledging it.

The more black women we can get to be easy going, the easier it will become for the rest of us to duck the stereotype. A select few of you make the rest of us look bad. Remember, the things you do to some will directly reflect onto all other black women so keep your boisterous behaviors, raging tempers and judgmental comments under control.

Just for fun I have created a test to rate your level of Angriness".

ARE YOU AN ANGRY BLACK WOMAN QUIZ

Check the letter, (a), (b) or (c), that most reflects the way you would behave in the situation. You can evaluate your answers at the end of the section.

1. You're driving on the freeway and someone cuts you off, causing you to slam on your brakes. You...

    a) Scream loudly and honk your horn.
    b) Shrug your shoulders and keep driving.
    c) Hit the gas to catch up, ride beside them cursing and throwing threats.

2. You're in a restaurant and the server trips and spills a plate on you. You...

    a) Start cursing them, call them names and question their very right to exist.
    b) Tell the server it's okay and go to the bathroom to clean off.
    c) Ask for the manager and request dry cleaning and a comped meal.

3. Your best friend tells you that she just got engaged and informs you that she will be getting married on the day you've been planning your birthday party.

a) You tell her great and start planning the dress shopping.
b) You feel hurt because she knew it was your birthday and you plan your birthday party on the same day as her wedding anyways.
c) You plan to celebrate your birthday at her reception since you both have a lot of the same friends.

4. You see your ex-boyfriend at the mall and he's with a new girl. You...

a) Say hello to your ex and roll your eyes at his new friend, talking trash under your breath as you walk away.
b) Say hello and introduce yourself to the new friend and tell her it was great meeting her.
c) Try to avoid walking past them, to avoid awkwardness.

5. A friend agrees to help you move some boxes. While moving, he drops one and breaks all of your new kitchenware. You...

a) Tell him it's okay and thank him for helping you move in the first place.
b) Tell him that he owes you 19.99 for the broken glasses and continue to remind him for the duration of the move.
c) Help him pick up the box, take it to the trash and secretly hope that he offers to pay for it.

6. You are single because...

    a) There has not been anyone good enough, because all men are losers.

    b) You have not been dating due to your "work or school schedule".

    c) You are enjoying dating, but there hasn't been anyone that you have been compatible with.

7. While looking for parking, you find a spot at the same time as someone else coming from the other direction. You...

    a) Use judgement and decide, if the spot is on your side, you take it, but if it on the opposite side, you wave for them to take it.

    b) Pull into the spot as fast as you can, honking your horn if you see them move an inch.

    c) Drive past and allow the other person to have the spot.

8. You are in a clothing store and a woman grabs the last shirt that you had your eye on. You...

    a) Let her know that you had been looking at the shirt, tell her it's yours and demand that she give it to you.

    b) Pretend it didn't happen and find another shirt similar to it.

    c) Ask a clerk to call around to other stores to see which has the shirt in stock.

9. Your child's father is running late picking him up for his weekend visitation. You...

    a) Wait around until he gets there.
    b) Move on with your previous plans and let him know where he can pick up your child.
    c) You put the child in to hiding, and don't pick up your phone.

10. You have a live in boyfriend and you come home to a beautiful woman sitting on your couch. You...

    a) Talk directly to your boyfriend and ask, "Who is this tramp?"
    b) You say, "hello" and introduce yourself to her.
    c) You walk in, see her and then leave.

ANSWERS

1. You're driving on the freeway and someone cuts you off, causing you to slam on your brakes. You...

   a) Mildly Upset Mocha
   b) Meditation Mama
   c) Angry Black Woman

2. You're in a restaurant and the server trips and spills a plate of spaghetti sauce on you. You...

   a) Angry Black Woman
   b) Meditation Mama
   c) Mildly Upset Mocha

3. Your best friend tells you that she just got engaged and informs you that she will be getting married on the day you've been planning your birthday party.

   a) Meditation Mama
   b) Angry Black Woman
   c) Mildly Upset Mocha

4. You see your ex-boyfriend at the mall and he's with a new girl. You...

   a) Angry Black Woman
   b) Mildly Upset Mocha
   c) Meditation Mama

5. A friend agrees to help you move some boxes. While moving, he drops one and breaks all of your new kitchenware. You...

    a) Meditation Mama
    b) Angry Black Woman
    c) Mildly Upset Mocha

6. You are single because...

    a) Angry Black Woman
    b) Meditation Mama
    c) Mildly Upset Mocha

7. While looking for parking, you find a spot at the same time as someone else coming from the other direction. You...

    a) Mildly Upset Mama
    b) Angry Black Woman
    c) Meditation Mama

8. You are in a clothing store and a woman grabs the last shirt that you had your eye on. You...

    a) Angry Black Woman
    b) Meditation Mama
    c) Mildly Upset Mocha

9. Your child's father is running late picking him up for his weekend visitation. You...

    a) Meditation Mama
    b) Mildly Upset Mocha
    c) Angry Black Woman

10. You have a live in boyfriend and you come home to a beautiful woman sitting on your couch. You...

    a) Angry Black Woman
    b) Mildly Upset Mocha
    c) Meditation Mama

Now, tally your totals and see whether you are a Meditation Mama, a Mildly Upset Mocha or a raging Angry Black Woman.

MEDITATION MAMA

Sista, you are far too relaxed! Put the marijuana blunt down and notice the people walking all over you. Remember, your time and your feelings deserve respect. Speak up for yourself in a respectful and considerate manner to voice your opinions and thoughts.

MILDLY UPSET MOCHA

Great job! You are upset at appropriate times. You are strong and you show it in your ability to communicate and negotiate. As a Mildly Upset Mocha you will forgive and move forward. The right button can be pushed to cause you to be called an "Angry Black Woman" but, when that time arises, most likely it was warranted. Afterwards, you will move on with grace and poise.

ANGRY BLACK WOMAN

Girlfriend, you need to relax! Not everybody is against you nor are they doing things just to spite you. Stop being so quick to jump to conclusions of the worst kind. If your voice is too loud your point will get lost in the blabber.

Learn to understand your feelings and emotions so that you may adequately express them. If not, you will push healthy and positive people away.

Although this quiz was made for fun, you can use it to take a look at other ways the same situations can be handled. Can you sass up your quiet demeanor? Can you water down your fiery rages? I believe life should be lived in a balanced manner for full enjoyment of what this life has to offer, that's why I'm proud to say that I am Mildly Upset Mocha!

I remember being told in the early years, after high school, "Niki, I always had a crush on you in high school," I said, "Well, why didn't you ever ask me out?" He told me, "Because I thought you would roll your neck and say, HELL NO! I'm not dating a white boy! I just thought you would reject me and embarrass me."

It wasn't me that had the attitude. It was the black women he would watch on TV at that time. It made him believe that I was capable of more attitude than he had ever witnessed me having.

His words were good to hear. As I grew older and started becoming more interested in white men, I always thought of his comment when white men would show interest in their weird, non straightforward manner. I remember my friends words and know that they are interested, just scared.

White men will talk to a black woman, until the cows come home, before they will ever ask her out. They will even be your friend for many years without ever expressing their feelings for you.

This dialogue is from 2003, Bringing Down the House, where Howie Rottman (played by Eugene Levy) plays a wealthy business man who loves a Sistah, Charlene Morton (played by Queen Latifah).

The reason this script is so funny is because this will RARELY happen in the real world.

Howie Rottman:
I'd like to dip you in Cheez Wiz and spread you all over a Ritz cracker, if I'm not being too subtle.

Charlene Morton:
Boy, you some kinda freaky!

Howie Rottman:
Oh, you have no idea. You got me straight trippin', boo!

In a typical situation the black woman will have to be the one to make it easier for a white man to approach her. Here are a few tips to make sure you appear open and approachable.

THE APPROACH

TIP #1
STAY IN HIS SIGHT

First things first, when you see the white guy that you like, get your group of girls together and station yourselves within a couple of steps of him. You want to stay in his eye sight. That way you have made it easier for him to approach you. Of course, don't make it obvious. Just pretend that you and your friends were walking towards the restroom and, all of a sudden , you have to fix your shoe. Now everyone stops walking and starts a conversation. Keep your friends in the "know" about what you are trying to do so they don't get confused. Otherwise, they'll wonder why you're talking about a bunch of random stuff while fixing your shoe.

During the conversation make sure you position yourself in his line of sight. Also, make sure that he sees you checking him out. When your eyes lock, throw him a smile. By now, even though he may till be a little shy, he knows that you are interested.

I personally like to lead the horse to water, pull its reins so his mouth touches it just to make it easier for him to drink.

TIP #2
YOU MAY HAVE TO
TAKE THE FIRST STEP

So now that you have lured your white guy over to you and introduced yourselves, you may find that you're stuck in a long conversation. Where do you go from here?

Many of my girlfriends tell me that they aren't sure if the guy was interested, or if he was just being nice and engaging in conversation out of politeness. My simple guideline is that he is interested if:

* You are talking for 5 minutes and he hasn't mentioned a wife or a girlfriend.
* He offers you a drink. He is gazing at your body and eyes. (It's a look that says he may kiss you at any moment.)
* He keeps a steady smile.
* He is engaged in the conversation.

Begin asking pertinent questions to show your interest in him. Ask him about where he comes from and his relationship status. When doing this, I like to add a touch to stimulate his senses. A glide or a pat on the his arm while laughing seems to do the trick. If he still is quivering in his boots, I tend to be very straight forward and say, "Well, I really have to get out of here." Even if I don't really have anywhere to go. Then I say, "Why don't you take down my number and call me some time."

Make sure that you give him your number. The importance of this is to establish the fact that you want him to take the lead in the relationship. If you don't, you will find yourself taking charge of everything related to you both. If you allow him to be in control from the beginning, you are letting him know that this will be the expectation from this point forward. Even though, ultimately, we will step in and give a hand here and there.

Men like to chase. So let him!

TIP #3
CLOSING
THE CONVERSATION

Most white men will need a helpful nudge at the closing of a conversation. White men who date black women enjoy the give and take of control. They appreciate the fact that they don't have to be the leaders all of the time. So, you giving him your number puts the "leadership ball" in his court and still allows him to feel masculine.

Keep in mind that if you find a white guy who closes the conversation successfully on his own, you have found a guy who has probably dated a black woman before and feels comfortable with taking charge of a relationship with one.

Sometimes, the white man may not close the conversation the way you would like because he isn't interested. I'm not saying that he's not interested in

all black women. You just might not be the right fit
for each other. It's up to you to watch for those cues.
Remember though, that there is a difference between
being flirtatiously straightforward and obnoxiously
aggressive. I have compiled a list of common hints that a
man is not interested.

WARNING SIGNS
A MAN IS NOT INTERESTED

* He avoids direct eye contact.
* He doesn't seem to be focused on the conversation.
* Look for the nod out (The moment your talking,
  he will nod and slowly start turning their head away
  from your direction).
* He gives you his BBM, Email, FaceBook page
  instead of an actual phone number.
* He will keep texting during your conversation and
  MAY even make/answer a call.

These are signs that he may not be calling. If he does
any of these things, don't stay up all night waiting by the
phone. Move on and push forward. There is a white
man out there for you!

TIP #3
LOCK AND LOAD WITHOUT DISTRACTION

Jason, 32 years old, was at a nightclub where an astonishing African American woman caught his eye. He wasn't quite sure how he would talk to her, but knew that he wanted to. As she strolled to the dance floor he sat pondering what his first words would be. There, a black man walked up to her and they began to dance.

Instantly, Jason began making excuses about why he couldn't ask her out. First, he assumed that she didn't like white guys. Secondly, if she liked white men, he couldn't talk to her because that black man was probably her boyfriend. His insecurity of racial rejection had kicked in!

The problem here is that once a white man sees you and a black man talking, exchanging numbers and having a drink, it will automatically build their insecurity of racial rejection and, even though they were very interested, they will never approach. You have now become an unattainable object.

In no way am I saying to ignore the brothas. What I am saying is that if you are not interested in him, keep the conversation brief and don't accept an offered drink. An extended conversation WILL affect your chances with the white men in the room.

Your best bet would be to go to the "whitest" nightclub in your town, grab a group of your non-judgmental friends for a girls night out and have a great time.

Find the men in the room that you're interested in and show yourself as available by engaging in eye contact and smiles. Once you have started a conversation with an interested party, make sure that you always close the deal.

If you have a few men lined up:

* move on to Chapter 5, where I walk you through the date.

If you still do not have any prospects:

* go back to the previous 4 chapters and see what you may be doing wrong.

Chapter Five

Rules for Dating a White Man

"Dating should be less about matching outward circumstances than meeting your inner necessity."
—Unknown

RELAX....
IT'S JUST A DATE

*C*ongratulations, you've found your location, made eye contact, maneuvered through the conversation, closed and got the date! Now, there are going to be certain situations you may encounter that can make or break future dates and the possibility of your moving forward into a relationship.

As black women, we think of dating white men differently than dating black men. We tend to treat them differently and have different expectations. We should recognize that they may also have the same dilemma when dating a black woman. They might have certain expectations of us.

The first date can be pretty nerve wracking to think about. You will have to figure out what to wear, what to order, what to talk about and how you can possibly keep the white people jokes to yourself.

There may be certain subject areas that you are nervous about so I've established some rules and simple guidelines to help steer you away from the mistakes that my friends or I have made in the past. I will give you the important tools that work when dating a white man.

RULE #1
DO NOT TAKE ADVANTAGE.

Many black women think that dating a white man means you are getting into a relationship where you will be able to walk all over him. If that's the case, get out now or he will leave you later. Yes, we get a lot further than we could with a black man, but don't take advantage. White men who date black women are the type that like more give and take when it comes to dominance in the relationship. They don't want to be the leaders all of the time. They want a partner.

According to a few white men I've spoken to that date black women, the ability to take charge is one of the attributes that they say they like the most. They love a black woman's independence and ability to take control when needed. These are not the men looking for a passive type of woman who they need to explain everything to.

In the same breathe, however, those same men will tell you that this attribute also doubles as the one they hate most about black women. For one reason or another many of us have had to take the lead in our own lives. Either our parents were working full-time jobs and we were held with more responsibility than an average child, or maybe we've been living on our own and supporting ourselves for a long time. Either way, it's difficult to allow someone else to have a turn in directing your life.

If you try to overpower your white guy too often you will begin pushing him away. White men have a strong level of patience when it comes to the people that they care about. You might succeed for a while but don't slip into the habit of always being in control. Take turns when it comes to decisions. Let him get in a word when arguing or in a debate. Respect him and his thoughts. Let it be a partnership.

A man of any type, is still a man, and needs to be treated as such.

RULE #2
DROP THE ATTITUDE AND RELAX!

Like most men, this category of men love to feel as though they are teaching you something new or showing you something different. For dates, they could choose locations such as museums, plays, operas, and unique cuisines. Yes, you will also get your standard date, but a white man is more likely to try to make your date an experience you'll remember.

During your experience, try not to "one up" your date. If you've been to the museum multiple times, and know every exhibit like the back of your hand, you don't have to act like it. As he's giving you facts, whether right or wrong, realize that he's trying to impress you and don't cut him down at the knees.

One difference between black women and white women is that white women are more passive. That is not to say that they are stupid. It's actually just the opposite. They realize that to get a guy wrapped around their finger they have to appear as if they are wrapped around his. White women seem vulnerable and the men love the feeling that they can help. Whether or not the men are wise to what is really happening doesn't seem to make a difference. They would love to have that quality in a black woman.

You will have to relax a little and be open minded when dealing with this type of man. These men come from a spur of the moment, go with the flow, sort of culture. If you want to enjoy yourself and go on a ride like no other then you must be the same way. Really work on doing your best in this area. You will experience a life you've never imagined. That said, make sure you have a passport. White men like to travel on a whim!

RULE # 3
NEVER SWEAT OUT YOUR HAIR ON A FIRST DATE!

I was a former basketball player in my town, and one time, I had an offer on a first date to go play. The first thing that came to mind was my hair. I had to tell him,

"I'm sorry, it's too early in our dating relationship to go there."

This is the one area, I think, where we are allowed to be a little more uptight. First of all, our hair takes numerous hours and a couple days after washing to get exactly how we like it. The last thing we want to do is mess it up for a first date. That may not go well.

Before I go out with a man, I ask myself,

"IS HE WORTH ME DOING MY HAIR?"

The next question is, "Is he worth messing up my hair?" For a first date, the answer is always, NO.

The second problem with sweating out your hair too soon is the white guys understanding of what we have happening up there. Many won't know what's happening when your edges start reverting and curling up. Unless you have a portable flat iron, or the right product to go to curly style, stay away from sweat or any other moisture.

White men that have not dated black women before do not understand our hair and the first date is not really the place to discuss it. You will find yourself getting upset at the the words they use so just save yourself the drama. It'll be a lot easier for you to understand where his questions are coming from after a few dates.

Being a black woman with with the option of natural locks, I always have hard time figuring out what style to wear it. I have noticed that each type of white man likes their women's hair in certain styles. The businessman prefers long straight "barbie" hair. Preferably, 16" or longer. He will accept you when you change it up later and he already cares for you, but upon first interaction their eyes focus on the long hair, whether the woman is black or white.

Edgy dudes like natural, hip and trendy styles. With the edgy dude they will be attracted to hair with odd and fun colors, short bobs or even completely shaved. If they find it unique they want it. I once had half of my hair shaved and had designs added in and during that time, I had never had so many edgy white guys hitting on me.

Your jock will go either way and will like you however you are. Although, upon initial attraction they like the woman with the straighter hair. But a fro won't scare them away.

Now, let's say that you have a weave or tracks hidden in your hair. It would be a prudent to let your man know because, WHITE MEN ARE HAIR PULLERS! I wouldn't disclose that information in the first date, but definitely before the first kiss, because a hand full of Polynesian wavy wouldn't be sexy to him. In intimate situations, their hands are like magnets to the scalp.

Corey, a 28 year old white male, recalled experiencing his first weave incident when I asked him to tell me a funny story about dating a black woman. They had just finished a date and he went in for the kiss. As his hand went into her hair, the only thing he kept thinking was, Did she get into a horrible accident? That scar is pretty wicked! So he asked her, "What happened?" Her response, "Oh! It's a Weave!" Which confused the poor little white boy even more. He had no idea what a weave was and why it would make someones hair so bumpy.

The way I see it is, they are either going to accept you with the fake hair or they wont. Just be up front. When a guy compliments my hair, I just say, "Yeah, I like it, too! That's why I bought it. I'm glad we have the same taste." We laugh and move on.

When things get really serious, there may be a time he will see you without your fake hair and your locks at their natural state. This is when you rent the documentary"Good Hair", by Chris Rock and have movie night. It goes through all of the processes black women go through to make their hair manageable whether curly or straight, real or fake.

Corey, who I mentioned earlier, stayed up watching movies late one night and sat through the Chris Rock documentary.

"I had no clue about what you guys go through. It's mind blowing, how in the dark I was!"

Although, not all white men are naive when it comes to our luscious locks. I've had one man approach me, who carried a Masters Degree in Sociology, say "That's an awesome hat! But, I know you didn't wear it because of a fashion statement, you're wearing it because of the rain!" He followed this with a flirtatious chuckle.

At first I was in shock because of his knowledge about our hair issues. It threw me off guard. But that let me know he's had black women in his life and that I could possibly sweat my hair out with him early on.

White men will vary on this topic but, until you know their level of knowledge, stick to the rule!

RULE #4
BE A CULTURED DINER.

When I mentioned being "open-minded" I meant several things but it is dining where it will benefit you the most. Open your pallet to new and exciting foods that you may not have eaten before. Your white man may take you places that you are not familiar with where you may discover loves for foods that you may have never thought you'd enjoy.

ETIQUETTE

There are many ways to dine depending on culture but there are a few basics when it comes to etiquette that every woman in America should know.

By now you should know:

* you don't talk with your mouth full
* keep your elbows off of the table
* place your napkin on your lap
* don't start eating until everyone has received their plate

However, there are a few other specifics that I feel should be added. Here is a list of them, based on personal experience, which you should be aware of.

1. Which piece of silverware do I use?

If you are seated and notice that there are more utensils than you're used to, have no fear. All you do is work from the outside in, towards the plate. At finer dining establishments each course will have it's own piece of silverware. At less fine locations you're stuck waving down the waiter that took your fork away with the salad and never returned with a new one.

2. You take a bite of food and notice a bone or shell in your mouth or the food doesn't taste right.

If you need to remove a piece of food from your mouth the rule is that you must do it in the same way that it got there. This means that if you took a bite using a fork then you'd remove it with a fork. If you took a bite using your hands, you remove the item with your hand. Place it on the side of your plate.

3. You have to use the restroom during the meal.

When nature calls in the middle of dinner, make sure you excuse yourself from the table without announcing that you're going to use the restroom. Just say, "Excuse me". Don't place your napkin on the chair, which is gross when you think about it. Place your napkin on the left hand side of your plate.

4. You have finished eating and you are ready for the server to take the plate.

When you are ready to order dessert and the server hasn't removed your dinner plate it may be because your utensils have not been placed in their proper positions. When you are finished, place your utensils face up at the four o'clock position on your plate. Make sure that your knife blade is facing inward. Keep in mind that once you start eating it is considered rude for a used piece of silverware to touch the table cloth. When you are finished with the meal leave the napkin, neatly and loosely, to the lefthand side of the plate. Never ball it up.

5. You're not sure what an item on the menu is or what to order.

As women, we luck out in this area because, traditionally, the man is supposed to order for you. Hopefully he did his research and knows the restaurant favorites. He should also ask you what kind of foods you prefer and which ones you don't care for so he can then order accordingly. I find that this can be a relief when I have never dined at the establishment and feel overwhelmed by the menu. If the guys don't take the lead, when they ask what I want my response is, "I'm not really picky and I trust your judgment."

On the other hand, if you have been to the restaurant before and you are craving that certain dish, let him know what you want and he can then relay it to the waiter.

MEAT

When visiting a steakhouse, your date may order it rare or medium-rare. You should try the same. If you're a "well-done" type of girl, start at medium-well and move on down to less and less brown. You'll be amazed at how juicy and tender a medium-rare steak is.

Here are the different levels of preparation for steak:

RAW

★ Uncooked. Used in dishes like steak tartare.

SEARED, BLUE RARE OR VERY RARE

* Cooked very quickly; the outside is seared, but the inside is usually cool and barely cooked. The steak will be red on the inside and barely warmed.
* Usually the chef will put the steak in an oven to warm up the inside. This method generally means that 'blue' steaks take longer to prepare than any other steak, as these require additional warming time prior to cooking.

RARE
(52 °C [125 °F] core temperature)

* The outside is grey-brown, and the middle of the steak is red and slightly warm.

MEDIUM RARE
(55 °C [130 °F] core temperature)

* The steak will have a fully red, warm center.

MEDIUM
(60 °C [140 °F] core temperature)

* The middle of the steak is hot and red with pink surrounding the center. The outside is grey-brown.

MEDIUM WELL DONE
(65 °C [150 °F] core temperature)

★ The meat is light pink surrounding the center.

WELL DONE
(71 °C [160 °F] and above core temperature)

★ The meat is grey-brown throughout and slightly charred.

OVERCOOK
(much more than 71 °C [160 °F] core temperature)

★ The meat is dark throughout and slightly bitter.

Other foods have different requirements. Pork should be prepared medium to medium-well and duck should be medium-rare due to the fact that it gets really tough.

You will have an option of how well to prepare just about any meat. Many times the most appetizing way to go is the way the chef suggests. Don't be afraid to ask, "What does the chef recommend?" That's how I found out these little tips!

WINE

When ordering your wine, remember, don't order by the color. Wine is not Kool Aid! I have noticed that, whether in public or with family, blacks have a very low appreciation of wine. The wines we like are typically white and very sweet. There are many other wine options other than the sweet ones.

Beautiful couple
David Reinprecht and Yvonne Cheri.

Black girls, please start expanding your wine pallet and learn which wines would be a good pair with the meal of choice. You should be looking for the optimal taste pairing in your mouth.

I will go through the main wines that you will recognize on your wine list. There are many more, but I will leave that up to you to taste and play with.

Remember, everyone has a different taste preference. This is just a starter lesson for my beginners.

You will typically drink white wines while enjoying a light appetizer, salad or a non robust main course. They are also great on hot days because they are always served chilled.

POPULAR WHITES

Grape	Tasting Notes	Pairing
Chardonnay (shar-dun-aye)	Toasty, buttery, citric flavors	Seafood/Poultry
Riesling (ree-sling)	Flowers/tropical fruits	Pork/white fish/ salty foods
Sauvignon Blanc (saw-vin-yawn blonk)	Melon, citrus, passion fruit	White Meat/Shellfish
Moscato d'Asti (mo-ska-toe de aw-stee)	Rich, sweet , sparkling	Cheeses and chocolate desserts

When ordering a more robust meal, like heavy meats, red sauces and any other dish with a lot of flavor it is time to order a red wine. Here is a list of popular red wines that you will commonly find on your wine list.

POPULAR REDS

Merlot (great for beginners) (mur-low)	Dark berry, gentle	Tenderloin/Lamb/ Grilled foods
Cabernet Sauvignon (ca-bur-nay saw-vin-yawn)	Full bodied,	Red Meats/
Malbec (mal-bec)	Wood-like rustic	Red meats/ mexican/ cajun/Indian
Pinot Noir (pee-no nwar)	Delicate, fresh, fruity	Grilled Salmon/ Chicken/ Lamb
Syrah/Shiraz (sir-ah/ shee-raz)	Hearty, spicy, black pepper	Steak/Stew/ Wild Game

I love to drink Moscato d'Asti by the pool on a hot summer day. It's sweet, crisp and fun for drinking with the girls. However, as much as I love it, I won't order it with robust foods. With those I would prefer a glass of Cabernet or something bold from the Bordeaux region. Bordeaux rarely comes by the glass so, if you have a chance to order it, build your meal around it.

SUSHI

Another place your date may take you to is a Sushi restaurant. Again, be open minded. I've been complimented by multiple white men on my love for sushi, because many of their black dates would never go for it.

If you aren't sure about what type of fish you like, there are always the standard sushi rolls that you can choose from. Some of my favorites are the Rainbow Roll, Spider Roll and Spicy Tuna Roll.

To not look "tacky", unless it's in combination with a more delectable dish, stay away from the California Roll. It's very cliché for blacks to order the simple rolls, just as we do the sweet wines.

If it's your first time you should also try nigiri-zushi aka "Sushi", which is a slice of raw fish on vinegar rice. I would recommend Yellowtail or Blue Fin Tuna. Neither taste fishy and it's an easy way to step into the Japanese way of dining.

Maybe you're nervous about using chopsticks. Well you're in luck. Japanese restaurants will often give you a warm towel at the beginning of your meal to wash your hands because, when consuming the Nigiri-zushi (sushi), its OK to use your fingers. But if you decided to order sashimi, which is simply sliced raw fish, it's time to get those sticks clicking.

Try and have a good time. If you're too nervous, you can always order a bottle of Sake to loosen you up!

RULE #5
BE KEEN ON CULTURES/
DON'T BE A RACIST.

As blacks, we tend to make comments and jokes about white people all of the time but, as soon as they say one thing about us, we scream racism. Keep in mind that what you say can hurt white people as well. Blacks can be ignorant racists too.

Black Girl:
Are you white or are you Jewish?
White Boy:
Are you Black or are you Christian?

This dialogue happens often to my guy friend when first meeting black girls. He told me that they look confused when he responds, "Jewish is not a race it's a religion!" There are black Jews, too!

When dating white men, you will meet men from all different cultures, religions and beliefs. Where I live, a large portion of those white men are Jewish. Many Jewish people fought along with Christians, Muslims and Baptists on the quest for freedom and desegregation.

I have a number of outstanding, sweet and generous Jewish male friends. In fact, since I've moved to Los Angeles I have considered many of them to be my extended family. We have a running joke where we say that the reason we have so much in common is directly related to the fact that we both come from oppressed peoples. We know how to make "something" out of "nothing".

Jewish men have strong family values and will bend over backwards for a friend in need. They have a keen knowledge for business and many are successful entrepreneurs.

When meeting a Jewish man there is one big determining factor, of how long your white man/black girl relationship will last. It could depend on the man's involvement with the synagogue and your willingness to choose, study and convert to a religion that you may know nothing about.

If you are a black Jewish woman you will have no problem here. But for others it's easier to talk earlier on, weighing your options, and decide if you should keep pursuing each other.

Do keep in mind, Jesus was a Jew!

RULE #6
EXERCISE AND STAY FIT.

"I saw a woman wearing a sweatshirt
with "Guess" on it so I said,
"Thyroid problem?"
—Arnold Schwarzenegger

Health and fitness is an area where a majority of us black women lack effort. I'll admit that I fall victim to this too. Although I will never buy pants a size larger.

When I notice my pants are not fitting correctly, I will go workout to get back to my normal size. Then, instead of making it a daily habit, I just stop once I've achieved my goal.

With heart disease and diabetes so prominent in the black community this is something we should be concerned about. According to the American Heart Associations "Statistical Fact Sheet" for 2007, 47.3% of black women were living with Cardiovascular Disease. 50,015 died of it in 2007 alone.

On a more important and superficial level we tend to let our curves get out of proportion. This is when those extra pounds migrate from that places we want them and position themselves into areas where we don't, like our stomachs, love handles and backs.

The number one thing that attracts white men to black women is our curves. You can probably guess which ones. But there comes a point where too much addition to your natural curve becomes a turnoff and ruins the chance of your being in a relationship with a white man.

There are exceptions who love a size 18-24 but, let's be honest, a majority of the time you'd be the booty call on drunk late nights while his trophy wife attends all of the public events, poses for all of the family photos and gets the paychecks. Harsh, but true!

I've heard friends say, "If I were to date a white guy he'd better be good looking, wealthy and nice." The same applies to us. If they are going to date a black girl we'd better be good looking, have a good body and be slightly reasonable.

Many woman are not willing to take care of their bodies and their own health for themselves so if a certain man is your motivation... get motivated! Hopefully it's a guy at the gym so you'll want to visit everyday.

Make healthier food choices, drink a lot of water and be active. Keep the curves tightly packaged without any extra rolls. We don't want your man to get sea sick from too much motion in your ocean.

Photographer Dan Hood and Model Ericka Harden

Now get out, go run and burn some calories!

If you're curious about how sex with a white man will be:

* Move on to the next chapter.

If you're following old school rules and holding off on sex until marriage then don't tease yourself:

* Move on to chapter 7 because it's time to meet his friends and family. Return to chapter 6 after you walk down the aisle.

Chapter Six

Sex
with
the White
Man

"What is commonly called love, namely the desire of satisfying a voracious appetite with a certain quantity of ***delicate white human flesh.***"
—Henry Fielding

SHOUT OUT...
TO THE IMPATIENT LADIES
WHO SKIPPED DIRECTLY
TO THIS CHAPTER!
(I SEE YOU)

*E*very black woman who's asked me a question about dating white men leads their questioning with concerns about sex. I imagine a great deal of you skipped directly to this chapter because you want to know;

"IS THE SEX GOOD?"

I am a black woman who loves sex and can admit it without feeling ashamed or feeling like I am at risk of condemnation. I have a strong sex drive and need someone that can keep up with me mentally and physically. I need someone that can fulfill my wildest fantasies and me, theirs.

So, I will answer that question with a truthful and honest, YES! The sex is great! It is the same as sex with a black man. Meaning that, while not ALL sex with a black man is great, you get more good ones than bad.

When having sex with a white man you are allowed to explore different sexual options. I find that with black men I am stuck into conventional sexual positions. They tend to stick with Missionary, Doggy style and Rodeo. For someone like me this can get quite boring. Yes, there have been a few that have been a little more fun but for the most part, that's it.

With white men I have tried positions and places like never before. On a wall, in a shower, in a forest, on a beach, nightclubs, jacuzzis, tables, kitchens, airplanes and anywhere else imaginable. We have disappeared into back rooms and hallways in the middle of parties and have done it, secretly, in a room full of people. White men are also more willing to implement toys to keep it fun.

White men have a strong sex drive and an even more imaginative sexual desire. They are also keen on making sure that you are satisfied first! When with a black woman, they will do what it takes for you to get to where you need to be before they do, as if they have something to prove.

The white man has been my perfect match sexually. A lot of black men will not *go down* on a woman until they have known her for awhile and it is a rare case to happen in a one night stand, which I have had a few of. With white men, however, *going down* is included in the sexual package. White men will let you know that they want to taste your pussy and nothing else. For them foreplay is a must. They do it because it turns them on and not because you asked. They do it because it's fun.

Black men also have a problem with me getting too exploratory and trying to put my fingertips in unfamiliar places. They think it makes them "gay" if they allow a girl to do it to them. If only they knew the pleasures that white men are comfortable with. They say that it feels good and, by the sound of their moans, they aren't lying.

This is a part of the *go with the flow* mentality of white men that carries over into the bedroom. They stay respectful and will never go further than you are willing to go, but will let you go as far as you let them go.

A great story that comes to mind is when Sheila met Pro Skater, Jereme Rogers. When they first met they had a long conversation and hit it off. The next time she met him out, with a group of friends, the two could not keep their hands off of each other. The sexual energy was too strong and both were willing to let their passion collide.

It started with kissing at a club. While sitting on his lap, she felt the size of his package through his pants and was even more aroused. Which was surprising because the guy was a little skate boarder dude who shouldn't have been packing like that. She had to let her friends see it. He was more than willing to show this group of black girls his oversized cock.

Next, before she knew it, she was giving him a blow job in the back of the club while her friends watched the door so that no one entered. The two were ready to go home and see what more would unfold. Because their passion couldn't wait, they began having sex in the backseat of the car while the friends watched and drove home.

Sheila went home with him and says that she had sex 6 times the next day and didn't make it home until 11pm the next night. She still remembers it as one of her best sexual experience ever. She let her insecurities go and had an experience she will always remember. Her and Jereme are still friends, and will continue to be, due to the love and trust they built in that single night.

BLACK WOMEN AND THEIR SEXUALITY

When asking the white men I surveyed about sex and black women, they responded with surprising responses. Because I am sexually open and willing to try new things, I thought all black women were like me.

Just like I mentioned black men and their being stuck to particular positions, white men said the same about black women. They said that we hate to *go down* and are stuck to missionary, doggy style and rodeo positions. When they try to flip them around into anything else, the response is, "Noooo!"

When asking how that differs from white women, the guys questioned said white women are always willing to *go down* and are more free with their sexual experiences. The guys I spoke with love sex with black women but they hate the struggle and how the women look at them when they try new things.

Backing my experiences and those of my white male counterparts, I found an excerpt from the CCIES at the Kinsey Institute:

[Regarding specific sexual behaviors, black men and women appear to engage in cunnilingus and fellatio less often than their white peers (Belcastro 1985; Hunt 1974; Laumann et al. 1994). A lack of foreplay is a grievance often expressed by married black women (Staples 1981), although black women report a higher frequency of intercourse per week than white women (Fisher 1980).

Another surprising difference that a white guy told me about is that more black women squirt than white women. Squirting can be defined as a female ejaculation that can be as much as 2 cups. It is not urine but liquid from the small female prostate gland. When the G-spot is aroused it causes a vaginal orgasm triggering the liquid to erupt. Many white men love to see this happen in person so don't be embarrassed when it happens. Just let it flow.

Things you can do to spice up your sex life with a white man is to buy toys such as these:
* Gigi (a toy that helps with hand jobs)
* Dildos
* Cock rings
* Butt plugs
* Bullets

You can also wear your sexy lingerie but, most of all, just let your fantasies be known. I guarantee there will not be anything that your white man won't try. As long as it is something that will turn you on... He's in!

SIZING HIM UP

We have all heard the rumors that white men aren't as big as black men when it comes to penis size. From personal experience I can say the rumor has no validity. In both cultures I've had both large and small, all averaging between the same lengths and girths. The smallest penis that I've been with did happen to belong to a white man but, then again, so did the biggest.

I also could never find a correlation between the height of the man and the size of his penis, no matter how hard I try to guesstimate. Often I find more shorter white men to pull out surprising packages as opposed to the taller ones.

If you look in the Guinness Book of World Records you will find that the award for biggest penis size belongs to a Mr. Jonah Falcon, with a penis measuring

9.5 inches when flaccid and 13.5 inches in length when erect! Yes... he is a white man!

According to the Kinsey Institute, men average 5–6.5 inches in length and 4–5 inches in girth. The studies have also indicated that 3.2% of white men are more predisposed to having shorter penises. This small amount throws off the race average for those guys with average sizers. And, because 13.6% of black men tend to have penises longer than 7 inches, it seems as though black men win in length.

When it comes to penis girth, white men take the lead. While 24.1% of white men participating in the study reported circumferences bigger than 5 inches, black men fell in at only 18.2%.

The problem with these statistics are that these numbers make us look at white men and assume that they have a small penis. When really, the odds of you getting a man in the miniscule 3.2 percentile is pretty slim.

Most men are in the same ballpark, but are you willing to let the white boys play?

Chapter Seven

Meeting the Friends and Family

"Treat people as if they were what they ought to be
and you help them to become what they are capable of
being."

—Goethe

"EXCUSE ME...
I WAS ON A SWIM TEAM,
THANK YOU!"

*N*ow that you've met, dated and hopefully are having a great successful relationship with your white man, there is going to come a time when he wants you to meet his friends and family. Not his hanging out buddies or the guy he works with, but his real friends. Maybe the ones he grew up with or the ones that he went to college with. The friends whose opinions really matter to him. This can be an awkward moment where you feel nervous, anxious and uneasy.

There are different perceptions the friends and family may have of you before they have ever met you. Thanks to the way we are portrayed on television, for whites that have not been around too many black people, the stereotypes that stick out in their minds are that all black women are loud, uneducated, can't swim and are from low income communities.

Not many people will voice these thoughts in public because it's taboo and they wouldn't want to be looked at as a racist, but they are real thoughts and there are ways to help ease their minds.

The first thing most white people think when they hear that their friend or son is bringing home a black girlfriend is, " OH SHIT" Followed by, "I hope that she has class." This usually isn't a thought when he's bringing home a white girl since they would automatically assume that most of them do.

There will be preconceived notions about you, and it's not that all of them are racist, they are just ignorant. It will become your job to be the voice and face of black people.

There will be a lot of barriers you will have to cross where that self control, self confidence and patience in yourself will need to grow.

TIP #1
COVER THE ASSETS

When first meeting the close friends and family you don't want to drop all of your curves on them at once. Cover up. You don't want mom to see dad checking you out across the dinner table. Don't give her more reasons not to like you. Don't wear the low cut blouse or the short edgy skirt. Even if you are dating the jock or the edgy dude, keep the style as if you were going out with the business man.

Depending on the function, I suggest a fun long loose fitted dress, or nice slacks. Wear nothing super fitted at all. Try to keep to a June Cleaver look. Mom will have nothing to say when you leave, other than, "She was a sweetheart". You know how we women are. No matter the age or race, we're going to find something wrong and gossip about it.

TIP #2
LEARN TO HOLD
YOUR TONGUE

Let me say this point blank, the white friends and family of your beau WILL say something that could offend you and your race. You will go through a slew of emotional feelings. The feelings of awkwardness, anger and sadness will leave you wondering, "do they even notice that I'm sitting here?"

Your first instinct as a black woman would be to jump up, cuss them out and let them know exactly what you think of them. Instead, when faced with these feelings in this situation, STOP, take a breath and consider your words wisely. Remember, you are the voice of ALL black people at this point, and unlike Jackie Chan in Rush Hour, they will hear the words coming out of your mouth!

You will always be the black girl that their son dated when bragging about their connection to black women. They'll say , "My son dated a black girl once...." and it's up to you on how the statement will end.

It all comes down to how you interpret their comments and how you will react. You have to consider media brainwashing, the way their friends and family were raised and their interactions with blacks. I would like to think that most people are not racist, just ignorant. Many have not had to think about what they say and how it may offend a black person. They are just used to speaking frankly because there had never been any black people around before you.

This is where you can help them with their future interactions with blacks. You can do this by recognizing what they are really trying to say and give them the correct phrases so they won't offend you, or anyone else, again.

When I've done this in the past, the whites had never realized that their words could be taken in such a negative manner. They apologize and change their perspective. Be willing to forgive and guide your man along with his friends and his family.

I remember hanging out in school with a group of my guys friends and one said,

"I hate black people." This is where the, "Does he see me standing here?" statement comes in. I then said to him,

"John, I'm black, if you haven't noticed." His response was a nonchalant,

"But you're a girl! I like the girls."

I pondered that statement for a minute before I responded with,

"So, if I had a brother, you wouldn't like him? Because he'd be just like me!"

Then, his response made his statement make sense.

"I don't like those black guys that hang out on the corner with their pants all saggy and they sit around talking shit."

"OH!" I said. "I agree, I don't like them either. But, you shouldn't go around saying that you don't like black people because of those idiots."

He realized that what he said was a bit harsh, apologized and we moved on.

TIP #3
SLACK ON THE
SALT

Its a known fact that whites and blacks eat different foods, or the same foods, just prepared completely different. You can bring a whole new culture to their world, and they to yours. This is where I think the saying, "Once you go black, you never go back", comes from.

When you first start cooking for your white boyfriend and his family, they may think that your food is a little too spicy and maybe a bit over seasoned and salty.

Remember, many white families will just buy the spaghetti sauce in a jar, warm it up and serve it. Black people will buy that same jar, add at least 5 different spices, meats, vegetables and let it simmer for an hour, as if we made the entire meal from scratch. This creates a different taste pallet between blacks and whites.

Blacks should cut back on all the salt, but once you've done it for so long, it's hard for your taste buds to revert back to the less strongly seasoned foods. (My nice way of saying bland).

Your man will love your dishes, if he can handle your obsessive infatuation with cayenne pepper and seasoned salt.

Although I have never experienced this, my girlfriend Alyssia told me a story about the one, and only, time she dated a white man. She recalls cooking for him, and every time, he would begin sweating profusely and begin to drink glasses and glasses of water. She didn't know how to help him. The spices that she used were just too much for the poor guy.

Eventually, his pallet toughened and he began to enjoy her meals. So there is hope.

TIP #4
PUMPKIN VS.
SWEET POTATO

For thanksgiving, and other holiday dinners, I have found the difference between the black families and white ones. I have been disappointed so many times that this topic deserved a place in my book.

Black families in America include greens and sweet potato pie to each holiday dinner. While the white families do a green bean casserole and pumpkin pie. For each, it's just not a holiday without them.

If you're planning a dinner at a white home, to where you've been invited, make sure to whip up a batch of your favorites and bring them over, that way you'll feel at home, and at the same time, they can get a taste of your culture.

If you're doing a holiday dinner for your white guy, make sure to include a dish that makes him feel like home, as well. We all love our family traditions and this is a little something that you can do to help him keep his. Or else, you may be stuck going to his family's home every holiday.

I can't say that I will ever make a green bean casserole, but I'll make sure there's a pumpkin pie on the table!

Once you have met the friends and family, you may be at the point that you are considering marrying your beau.

If you have children that you are considering introducing your white man to:

* move on to the next chapter.

If you don't have children but are considering marriage:

* skip to Chapter 9

If you are still in party mode, and not looking for a kid or marriage;

* skip to chapter 11

Chapter Eight

Black Kids and a White Man

"To me, my stepfather is so much more than just a parent; he made the choice to love me when he never had to."
—Julie Hébert

NO HONEY...
HE'S NOT REALLY YOUR UNCLE.

*M*any of us single black women have children and are powering through work, fun and parenting alone. We make sacrifices everyday to bring our children happiness, whether or not we are happy ourselves.

We yearn for our children to have a positive male role model that loves them and treats them with respect. We pray for someone to help teach and guide them throughout their lives.

When I had my first daughter, who is bi-racial, I was left caring for her with a man who was a father only when he wanted to be. When she turned two, I began a relationship with a man, who happens to be a child of a white man and a black woman. He stepped in as a father and accepted her as his own. Although, we have married and separated, he has not abandoned her and he still acts as her father. Well, in our case, *better* than a father, he is her DAD!

Throughout the years, and another daughter later, his entire family has taken in my daughter as a niece, granddaughter and even great granddaughter.

Grandma Helen, a white woman, at 86 years old, couldn't stop picking up and kissing my daughters when we made a visit to New York. They were her great granddaughters, black or white.

Of course, a white man who married a black woman in the times of harsh racism wouldn't have a problem, but I think that it should be noted that there are white families out there that love and accept blacks as their own family.

When first starting this book there was a question that a friend asked me that I never even considered. Being a mother of bi-racial children, I hadn't thought of what a white man would think when he is told the black woman had a darker skinned child. She asked me:

"WILL A WHITE MAN ACCEPT MY BLACK CHILD AS HIS OWN?"

I asked about ten white men this heartfelt question. I had concerns about their answers being truthful, for the mere fact that I, their friend, was a black girl with children, but their answers were well thought out and all were the exact same.

They all responded that if they really loved the woman, and they were going to make that choice to start a family, it wouldn't matter what color the child was, because a "kid is a kid". They are innocent and you can't help but to love them. The guys also mentioned that they would treat the child like their own, because if they were raising him/her, the child would be.

There are men that will want children between the two of you, if they don't already have any, but it wouldn't make them love your child any less. I don't believe that parents who adopt children love their biological ones more. Once you open your heart to anyone, the love is so strong that it can't be measured.

Asking a guy, black or white, to step into an already 'built' family unit is asking a lot of any man. Many single men aren't ready for that commitment. Because, when they're in a serious relationship with you, a mother, they are in a serious relationship with your child, too. This can be an overwhelming thought for some.

I have found that more white men in their mid-thirties, and up, are ready for that kind of commitment and responsibility. They have steady careers by now, a home and feel that they have something to offer a family. If a man is younger and still finding himself, this situation will make him feel inadequate and insecure.

MEET YOUR NEW DAD!

I hear women say, "My child has a dad, you don't have to be his dad!" That statement is far from the truth. The man you decide to date, will be a role model in his/ her life, whether you want it or not. They will look at how he treats you, how he treats them and it will effect who they become as adults. So, while you're still in the courting process and before you introduce your new beau to your children, keep in mind, your children will remember him.

I think about my mothers ex boyfriends regularly and hope they are doing okay. I've even considered finding them on internet just to say hello. Many have had impact on my life. Some were nice and some I couldn't wait for her to leave. I wished my mother could have worked out the relationship with them, but that wasn't the case. I can remember my mothers boyfriends all the way back to when I was in Kindergarden. So mothers remember... your child is being effected.

When dating, there comes a point when it's time to see how the man interacts with your children. I suggest to never introduce the men as, someone you're dating. Always leave them as a "friend" and go do something fun, like a movie or dinner. Don't show any intimacy, as a matter of fact, don't go within 3 ft of each other and leave all conversation at the friend level. Kids will pick up on the slightest of gestures. Although, I would refrain from having your kids use the term "uncle" because if it does work out, that could be difficult to explain.

When you return home, listen to their comments about what they thought of your guy. Children are great at reading people and will let you know if they like them or not. Really take their opinion into account, no matter how hard it is. Because in the long run, it may be for the best.

Since you have considered introducing your new man to your children:

* Move forward to the next chapter to discuss marriage.

Chapter Nine

The Interracial Marriage

"They just were in love with one another and wanted
the right to live together as husband and wife in Virginia,
without any interference from officialdom."
—Bernard Cohen,
Attorney of Richard and Mildred Loving

WEEZ MARRIED NOW!!!

*F*or centuries is was a crime, punishable by law for us to date, marry or have sex with white man. There is a story about a couple, a white man and a black woman, Richard Loving and Mildred Jetter, who fled the state of Virginia, just to be married. Five weeks after arriving back to Virginia, the couple lay sleeping in their bed and the Police broke in at 2 A.M and arrested the couple for being married.

Pleading guilty to the charge against them, the couple was sentenced to one year in jail. The sentence was suspended for 25 years "on the condition that the Lovings leave the State and not return to Virginia together for 25 years."

After many setbacks throughout a nine-year period, their case was heard before the U.S. Supreme Court which in 1967 decided unanimously in their favor. This historical event was called, Loving vs. Virginia.

Richard and Mildred Loving fought hard to change the law to allow interracial marriages to be accepted in their state and opened the door so that they may live legally in love.

We have come a long way since 1967, Black female/ White male marriages, in America, went from 26,000 in 1960 to 80,000 by 2000, according to the U.S. Census Bureau, and the numbers are expected to continually increase.

Joshua Denhardt and Stacey Newsome-Santiago

Growing up in California, I have experienced racism on a small scale, but for the most part, this state has become pretty relaxed when it comes to interracial unity. Here, if people are racist, they are too embarrassed to admit it in public. But, that was not always the case.

California's law on interracial marriage didn't happen until 1948 in the case of Perez v. Sharp.

As far as other small cities and countries, things may still be as they were in 1960's America, but remember that it took just a few people to change the lives of many others. You may have to fight, but if you love strong and stick together, you can overcome their ignorance.

If and when you decide to marry a white man, like any marriage, you will have to sit and discuss your goals, expectations and ethics with each other. Know that in some parts of the country, you will still get crazy stares, words and actions directed toward you. You may have to fight for your love, as those have before.

WHEN YOUR FAMILY DOES NOT APPROVE

I like to think that most black families love their daughters enough to accept their decisions when it comes to love. As long as that person treats them well and treats the family with respect. If your man doesn't, maybe you should find a new man. But if he does, you may have to consider sitting with your family for a heart to heart, and if they still don't accept them, you will be stuck making, probably one of the hardest decisions of your life. Your family or your man.

I can not help you make your decision, but what I could tell you is that, if I were ever put into that situation, I would have to make the decision to go with which person makes me the happiest, and causes the least amount of drama in my life. That said, if I had a family of racists, I could not entertain their thoughts, emotions and feelings, due to the selfishness, ignorance and absurdity of their thoughts. Hopefully, one day they would come to their senses and love me for me, whether they approve of my decisions or not, but until then, I would have to start my new family and my new positive future.

WHEN HIS FAMILY TREATS YOU WITH DISRESPECT

If his family is having a hard time coming to grips with the fact that their son is in love with a black woman, there is not much that you can do. All you can do is continue to be respectful and respectfully decline the invitations to be around them.

Don't jump to the conclusion that they don't like you because you are black, because it could be many other things. Maybe mom finds something wrong with every woman her son brings home, because he's a mamas boy. Maybe, he told her about an argument you had and mom blew it out of proportion.

But if it is, solely because of race, the only person that can do something in this situation is your man. He must sit with his family and explain that you will be together and that he demands that they treat the woman he loves with respect. If not, he will have to make a decision to honor his parents wishes or his own heart.

If you live in a populous city, chances are you will never get that rude, in-your-face, racist, mom of your new man. She may talk to him behind closed doors, but while you are around, she will fake it until her teeth hurt.

If you are in rural america, and you decide to stay in your town. You and your man may have to love your families from afar. You can't allow their negative energy to infect your relationship. If they have too much involvement, that is exactly what will happen.

I dated a man whose parents met in college in Alabama in the 70's. The father white and the mother black. They had a tough time with their relationship. The couple received threats of being hung on campus by the school's security because they fell in love.

Forty years later, they are still happily married, with four handsome sons and 3 grand-children. Sometimes it takes work to ultimately get what you want.

Just know that through your love you can have beautiful babies, blood or adopted, and raise them to be the loving and understanding people.

I have compiled a list of Black woman/ White man power couples and there were many more who didn't make the list.

* Kim Wayans (comedian, actress, writer, director& producer) and Husband, Kevin Knotts (sitcom writer, actor, writing partner)
* Chris Wineberg, Woman's coach and decathalon star, married to Olympian, Mary Wineberg. He gave up his Olympic dreams to help her to achieve hers.
* Naomi Campbell (Supermodel) and Russian tycoon Vladislav Doronin Producer
* George Lucas, Mellody Hobson (President of an investment company)
* Robert DeNiro (Actor, Director, Producer) and Grace HighTower (Actress)
* Robin Thicke (musician) and Paula Patton (actress) were high school sweethearts.
* Mats and Lydia Carlston (President of Nixon Peabody LLP, has a firm recognized as a Global 100 law firm)
* Congressman William Cohen may have some help with his speech writing from his author wife Janet Langhart.
* David Bowie and Iman (Supermodel)

This is just a few of many successful interracial couples, who have been married or dating for many years. The more we see and accept them in the spotlight, the easier it will be for interracial couples in small rural areas of the United States of America and across the world.

If your proposal or marriage idea didn't work out:

* Move on to the next chapter to refresh your memory of the guidelines, dust yourself off and try again.

If it's been awhile:

* Go back to Chapter 2 and see if you chose the right type of white man for you!

CHAPTER TEN

OPERATION "WHITE MAN" IS IN EFFECT

"Think ahead. Don't let day-to-day operations
drive out planning."
—Donald Rumsfeld

SO...
WHAT AM I SUPPOSED TO DO AGAIN?

*A*t this point, you've finished reading the lessons and now it's time to step out of the house and implement them. You may be a nervous wreck from just the thought of date a white man, or you may feel that you are a seasoned "white boy" veteran. In any circumstance, this book is here to be your guide through questions or issues that may come up. This book is to be implemented in conjunction with common sense and confidence.

Here is a quick rundown of what you have read and what you need to do in order to prepare you for your dates.

1. Make sure you look the part!

   * Natural makeup
   * Classy clothing
   * Be well Groomed
   * Work out regularly

2. Go where white men are!

   * Restaurants
   * Hole in the Walls
   * Nightclubs
   * Gyms and Country Clubs

3. Stay engaged!

   * Stay off of your phone.
   * Don't talk too much with friends

4. Be approachable

   * Give eye contact
   * Smile
   * Help with initial "Hello"
   * Help close the conversation

5. Be open minded

   * Try new food preparations
   * Try new sex positions and toys
   * Be willing to Learn

6. Cool down the attitude and judgments

* You are the voice of all blacks
* Be a teacher, when needed
* Don't be a Racist

7. Love and be loved

* Stand up for your love
* Allow your kids to be loved
* Be understanding

With these changes and additions to your life, your having a "Plus 1" to the party is right around the corner. Finding him should be a fun and interesting process for you and your girlfriends that want to take this journey with you.

When dating anyone, no matter the race, there will be up and downs. Everything we do and every decision that we make, is a learning lesson. Hopefully dating white men will allow you to learn things you may not have otherwise.

Now it's time to step into your heels and hit the scene! If you prefer house parties, consider throwing your own Racial Mashup Party where you can bring the interracial dating experience to your friends and loved ones. Your guide is for the party is one page away. Just make sure your black female guests have read the book first!

Chapter Eleven

Throwing Your Own Racial Mashup Party

"Don't be hatin'....We're only interracial datin'!"
—Niki McElroy

IF YOU WANT TO BE MY BABY, IT DON'T MATTER IF YOU'RE...

*N*ow that you've figured out that opening your options and dating outside of your race is easy and realistic, it's time to see if your friends are ready to join you. You'd be surprised on how many people have thought about it. So, what better way than to plan your own Racial Mashup Party.

This party isn't to say that the blacks and whites are required to only talk to the opposite race. It's to allow the comfort of knowing that everyone in the room is open to the idea of dating the opposite race. They are there to try it out.

ATTENDEES

Getting attendees to make an appearance at your Racial Mashup Party will be easier than you think.

The preface of your invite is to inform the invitees that everyone in attendance will have an open mind and be open for new, or continued, opportunities with someone of the opposite race.

You are cordially invited to

The
Racial Mash-up
Party

For those looking for love...
No matter their race

Time:
Place:

Come with an open mind and an open heart!

All are Welcomed!!!

RSVP to Niki McElroy @ 555-5555

After you've created you invite, contact your black female friends and let them know what you are doing, many will be excited to meet new men. If they have questions or concerns about dating outside of their race. Refer them to this book.

The key to getting the white men involved is by contacting a few of your white male friends. You can ask your co-workers, family friends and classmates to attend and bring their male friends that are interested in inter-racial dating. They will be excited to come to a place with single females and even more so because they're black females.

While adding names to your guest list, don't forget your white girlfriends and black men. Both of which are typically willing to date outside of their race and are a bit less closed minded than white men and black women.

Those that are a bit uncomfortable with the situation, this is either the time that they welcome themselves into the 21st century, or make sure that they stay home. You want your party to be fun and relaxed. You don't want any tension from the races, due to inconsiderate comments.

FOOD AND BEVERAGE

Once your invitation is made and mailed, it'll be time to start considering your theme and menu. Of course, a great theme for the night is a Black and White party. Where your guests wear black and white clothing, you decorate the room with black and white décor and the foods stick to a black and white theme.

DRINKS MENU

WHITE MAN

2 oz Bourbon Whiskey
Vanilla Coke

Pour Whiskey into a whiskey sour glass. Add 3 ice cubes, top with Vanilla Coke, and serve.

BLACK LADY

1 tsp Brandy
2 oz Orange liqueur
1/2 oz Coffee liqueur

Shake ingredients in a cocktail shaker with ice. Strain into a cocktail glass.

BLACK VELVET

5 oz chilled stout
5 oz chilled Champagne

Pour stout into a champagne flute. Add champagne carefully, so it does not mix with stout, and serve.

WHITE CHOCOLATE COFFEE FUCKER

1 oz Coffee Liqueur
1 oz Irish Cream

Put Kahlua in shot glass, layer Bailey's on top. Serve.

BLACK AND WHITE MARTINI

3 oz Vanilla Vodka
1 oz crème de Cacao

Pour the vanilla vodka and creme de cacao into a
cocktail shaker half-filled with cracked ice. Shake well,
and strain into a chilled cocktail glass. Garnish with
black and white licorice candy, and serve.

WILD WHITE SLIPPERY MUDSLIDE

1 1/2 oz Irish Cream
1/2 oz coffee liqueur
1/4 oz butterscotch schnapps
cream

Pour hershey's chocolate syrup around the inside lip of a
rocks glass. Fill with ice, add ingredients, and serve.

FOOD/APPETIZERS

POPCORN SERVED IN BLACK PAPER BOWLS

BLACK BEAN DIP WITH WHITE CORN CHIPS

CROSTINI WITH GOAT CHEESE AND A DOLLOP OF BLACK OLIVE TAPENADE

1 log goat cheese
1 can black olives, pitted
2-3 tbs olive oil
3-4 cloves of garlic, minced
In a food processor add garlic, olives and puree. As
the olives become pureed add olive oil in a drizzle to
combine.
Crostini
1 baguette, sliced
3 tbs olive oil
salt and pepper to taste

Brush slices of bread with olive oil and season with salt
and pepper. Place in a 300 F oven to toast. Remove
when browned. Spread Crostini with goat cheese and
Olive Tapenade.

MUSIC

When it comes to music, a eclectic playlist is what will be needed. If you're not sure what songs to add to your iPod, go with the top 40's of the last couple of years. Depending on age, you can also skip back quite a few years to include the oldies, but goodies.

If you are throwing your party away from home and in a local restaurant or bar, you may not have a decision on the music that will be playing. So, to help make everyone comfortable, choose your location wisely. Choose a place that already has a multiracial clientele, that way the tunes will remain diverse and the energy of the evening won't be invaded by unwanted stares of the uninvited restaurant patrons.

This along with an engaging host is all you need for this party to be successful. Your host should also play matchmaker if he/she see's two people that should meet and make sure everyone is relaxed and having fun.

For the women that are still skeptical of dating outside of your race due to America's violent history;

★ Move to the next chapter.

For the people ready to mix and mingle;

★ Get out and get to dating!

Thank you for letting me be your guide!

Chapter Twelve

(More than)
A
Few
Good
White
Men

"Change is the law of life. And those who look only to
the past or present are certain to miss the future."
—John F. Kennedy

NOT EVERYONE IS OUT TO HURT YOU!

*T*here are many black women that have an issue with
the idea of dating white men due to the history of the
blacks oppression at the hands of the whites. They feel
that it is "selling out" or a blatant disgrace to our people.
I hope this final addition to the book and help those
few of you over the issue. Remember, since slavery,
there have always been whites that had risked their lives
for blacks.

White men have always had an attraction to black
women, mostly not admitted. When forced to admit, the
white man blamed the attraction on the sexual energy
of the black female. Be it a myth or not, many white
men, over the course of centuries, have looked at being
with a black woman as taboo; as something they were
not allowed to do. It is human nature to desire what

we can't have. Therefore, white men longed for black women, more than anything.

Here is an excerpt written by Calvin C. Hernton from his writing on Sex and Race in America. Where he states;

"During the era of slavery... the white man had as much sex with the black women of his plantation as he did with his wife. Sometimes more. Lillian Smith, a white woman who was brought up in the South and is thoroughly familiar with its history, tradition, and secrets, writes:

> In the white southern woman's dictionary,
> Discrimination could be defined as a painful way
> of life which too often left an empty place in
> her bed and an ache in the heart. [Lillian Smith,
> Killers of the Dream 1963, p 125]
> Because his concept of the sex act made
> him think of it as something dirty, sinful, and
> savage, the white Southerner found it difficult to
> relate to his own woman. He was inhibited by
> the Calvinist interpretation of sex as befouling
> the dignity of man. He therefore cringed from
> his manly duties towards his wife, and if he did
> make love to her, the act was marred by his
> guilt and shame. . . . .Early during the period of
> slavery, light-skinned Negroes began to appear in
> the backyards of the great plantation houses of
> the South. As more and more of these 'mulatto'
> children began to run around in the backyards,
> guilt feelings fell upon the white man's conscience.

But the white man continued to visit, with increasing frequency, the black cabins. He stayed away more and more from the big house. Then there arose in him the suspicion of his wife left alone back there in the big house. The white man began to suspect his wife of doing exactly what he was doing. Of course, his suspicion was groundless, it was virtually impossible for white women to 'slip around' with Negro men during slavery. But somehow, someway, the white man had to get rid of his feelings of guilt. In jealous panic he projected his own transgression onto his women and onto the Negro male. A guilt so terrible seized the white man that it is as insane now as it was then -- devolutionary guilt." (Out of this came the Myth of White Womanhood.)"

Anne Braden, an American Advocate of racial equality, who led a delegation of southern white women organized by the Civil Rights Congress to Mississippi to protest the execution of Willie McGee, an African American man convicted of the rape of a white woman, Willette Hawkins states that "Because this kind of oppression--more than oppression, it was killing of black men. The excuse for it was to protect so called 'white womanhood.' The whole myth of white womanhood and the part that it played in the south at that time. So these white women-- this was long before my day; I don't think I ever really met any of them, but I read about them later and began to identify with that tradition--

were white women who said, "Thank you just the same, we'll protect ourselves. We're tired of being used as an excuse to kill black men."

We have read stories on our third president Thomas Jefferson and his love affair with his slave Sally Hemings, whose father was said to be John Wayles, Jefferson's father in-law. Although, there are no first hand accounts on the dynamics of the couple's relationship, the documents that have been proven thus far, leave us to come to our own conclusions. This leads me to believe that Jefferson fell in love with her, giving her six children, having her join him in France as his children's caregiver and bending the rules when first requesting that the maid who would come to France be inoculated. Jefferson brought Sally and paid for an expensive doctor to take care of her medical needs.

To me, Jefferson's story is one of many that clearly illustrates a white man's ability to love a black woman. Why is it hard for people to believe that white men can love black women? Do people not realize that love is greater than any law can dictate?

"A WHITE MAN HAS NEVER DONE ANY-THING FOR ME!"

Many black women have a problem dating white men due to the history of oppression and torture. Just as there were white men who raped and killed our ancestors, mostly because of their own fear and ignorance, there were those who loved and fought beside us, risking their own lives.

When Norman Cannon was found guilty of raping 15-year-old Rosa Lee Coates in Hattiesburg in 1965, it was the first time since Reconstruction that a white man had been convicted and sentenced to life in prison for raping a black woman. The attorneys representing Rosa Lee Coates were James Finch and James Duke, both white men.

Rosa Parks, who we know as a trailblazer to the civil rights movement, had a white attorney, Clifford Durr, bail her out of jail and take her case. He worked along the side of local attorney Fred Gray, for black citizens whose rights had been violated.

JOHN FITZGERALD "JACK" KENNEDY
(May 29, 1917 – November 22, 1963)

35th president during the 1960's Civil Rights Movement who helped pass laws to make sure all Blacks could vote and get a good education. These laws ended segregation in schools, jobs, restaurants, theaters, and more.

On Friday, November 22, 1963, in Dallas, Texas, Kennedy was assassinated.

JONATHON MYRICK DANIELS
(March 20, 1939-August 20, 1965)

Daniels with three others, a white Catholic priest and two black protesters, went to get a cold soft drink at one of the few local stores that would serve the non-whites. They were met at the front by an engineer for the state highway department and unpaid special deputy, who wielded a shotgun. The man threatened the group, and finally leveled his gun at the black sixteen year old Ruby Sales. Daniels pushed Sales out of the way and caught the full blast of the gun. He was killed instantly.

MICHAEL HENRY SCHWERNER
(November 6, 1939 – June 21, 1964)

Schwerner was one of three Congress of Racial Equality (CORE) field workers killed in Philadelphia, Mississippi, by the Ku Klux Klan in response to their civil rights work, which included promoting voting registration among Mississippi African Americans.

ANDREW GOODMAN
(November 23, 1943, – June 21, 1964)

Goodman was one of three American Civil Rights activists murdered near Philadelphia, Mississippi, during Freedom Summer in 1964 by members of the Ku Klux Klan. Their bodies were missing for nearly 2 months and made national headlines.

JAMES REEB
(January 1, 1927 — March 11, 1965)

Reeb was a minister from Boston, Massachusetts. As a Unitarian Universalist minister, Reeb was active in the Civil Rights movement, and encouraged his parishioners to do the same. With his wife and four children, he lived in poor black neighborhoods where he felt he could do the most good. While marching for Civil Rights in Selma, Alabama, he was murdered by segregationists.

REVEREND BRUCE W. KLUNDER
(1938 - April 7, 1964)

Reverend Bruce Klunder was a white Presbyterian minister and Civil Right activist, born in Oregon. He died at age 27 on April 7, 1964, when he was run over by a bulldozer while protesting the construction of a segregated school in Cleveland, Ohio. He was married with two young children. Klunder is one of forty individuals listed as a civil rights martyr on the national Civil Rights Memorial in Montgomery, Alabama.

GERMAN MENNONITE RESOLUTION

In 1688, and sixty-nine years after the first black slaves arrived in America, The German Mennonite Resolution, against slavery became the first formal protest of its kind. The "Resolution" opened the door for other anti-slavery groups but more importantly it made America and future Americans more conscious of the cause and its connection to freedom.

A question that I received from a girlfriend was, "Will a white man fight for you if someone is disrespecting you?" From this list of just a few of many strong, courageous white men, that were willing to die for what was right, there should be proof that there are ones that will stand behind their moral obligations and fight for what is right.

There have been many whites, men and women since the beginning of slavery that have helped fight for and work beside blacks. With the changing of society, now, many are willing to go further than ever before. So, don't let the past of some be indicative of your future with another.

Questions
and
Answers

Q: "I'm a little skeptical. Have you had a successful long-term relationship with a white man? Or are you just talking about getting them to sleep with you?"

A: Great question and one I have heard many times before. I first want to ask you a question.. Why is it that black women feel they aren't good enough for white men to love and if they are interested it is only because of an ulterior motive?

I know the answer, so no need to respond. But I just want to leave that thought for you and any other black woman thinking the same thing. We are beautiful and they want the opportunity to know us just as much as black men.

That said, yes I have had successful long term relationships and know many others who have, as well. I have not been married to a white man (due to my own unreadiness) but have made it to the meeting of friends and family of many of the white men I've dated. I have been asked to live with and have been asked to marry twice. I have white male friends married to black women, as well. I will have a couple write on my Facebook fan page and you can ask them questions that you may have.

Don't get me wrong, there are white men that want to have sex with black women because of the "intrigue" and may be looking for just that, but there are many black men looking for the same thing. That's what I wrote the book for. I want people to realize that there is no difference in the "wants" of a white man whether he's dating a white or a black woman. If he's looking for love, he's looking for love and if he's a douche bag he's a douche bag! We can't judge and entire race due to a few douche bags. If we were to do that to men of all races, there would be a whole lot of single women. :-)

Q: I was wondering, as a white non-american male, why would white men be appealing to black girls? Why would black beautiful woman choose this contrast of culture instead of familiar culture of another black man? What makes us different besides of the color of the skin?

A: There is no real "appeal" to dating white men, it's just about having more opportunities to find a good man. Although, studies have shown that more black women are graduating college than black men, leaving black women wanting to date someone at their own education level. So those ladies who not have considered it before are more likely to start opening their options. There is no difference besides the color of our skin and if the cultures are different that has nothing to do with what color you are, more about where you are from. If I were to date a black African man I would have a lot less in common than if I were to date a white American man from my town.

Q: Are there really singles out there having problems dating?

A: The answer is a big whopping YES!! People aren't finding lasting relationships that they're looking for becuase, most of the time, they aren't even sure about what they're looking for. I suggest to make a list of moral qualities that you need in a significant other and look for those and not just the outside appearance.

Q: I am a black woman and I never know if a white guy is hitting on me or just being nice. How can I tell?

A: I know it is difficult to determine if a man is interested. You should be confident enough to assume that they are. If not, there are some indicators that I will help ease your concerns.

* You are talking for 5 minutes and he hasn't mentioned a wife or a girlfriend.
* He offers you a drink. He is gazing at your body and eyes. (It's a look that says he may kiss you at any moment.)
* He keeps a steady smile.
* He is engaged in the conversation.

NOTES

NOTES

NOTES

NOTES

NOTES

NOTES